ANNABELLA BOSWELL'S
Journal

ANNABELLA BOSWELL'S
Journal

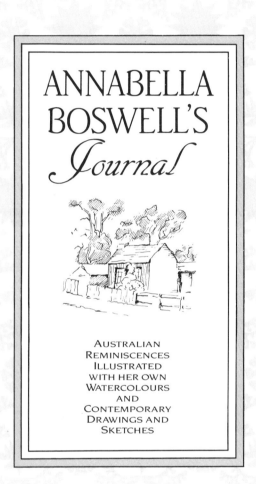

AUSTRALIAN
REMINISCENCES
ILLUSTRATED
WITH HER OWN
WATERCOLOURS
AND
CONTEMPORARY
DRAWINGS AND
SKETCHES

ANGUS
& ROBERTSON
PUBLISHERS

ANGUS & ROBERTSON PUBLISHERS acknowledge with sincere thanks the help of the Hastings River Historical Society in the publication of this Journal, both in its earlier editions and in this one which is embellished with Annabella Boswell's own watercolours of flowers. These watercolours, together with those appearing on pp. 55, 64–5 and 104–5 are in the possession of the Society and are used with their permission.

The black and white illustrations on pp. iii, 34, 48, 57, 67, 74, 87, 99, 108, 143, 159 and 187 come from the *Sketchbook of Emma Minnie Boyd* (1858–1936) now owned and recently republished by the National Gallery of Australia.

The illustration on p. 43 from the State Library of New South Wales is used with permission, as is that on p. 7 from the Mitchell Library, Sydney.

ANGUS & ROBERTSON PUBLISHERS

Unit 4, Eden Park, 31 Waterloo Road,
North Ryde, NSW, Australia 2113, and
16 Golden Square, London W1R 4BN,
United Kingdom

First published in Australia
by Angus & Robertson Publishers in 1965
This edition 1987
First published in the United Kingdom
by Angus & Robertson (UK) in 1987

National Library of Australia
Cataloguing-in-publication data.

Boswell, Annabella, 1826–1916.
  Annabella Boswell's journal.

  ISBN 0 207 15566 6.

  1. Boswell, Annabella, 1826–1916 — Diaries. 2. Women
  pioneers — New South Wales — Diaries. 3. New South
  Wales — Social life and customs. 4. New South Wales —
  History — Sources. I. Herman, Morton, 1901- . II.
  Title.

994.4'02'0924

Typeset in Bembo
Printed in Singapore

FOREWORD

ONCE AN AMERICAN President said that yesterday's newspaper is History. By this he inferred that its articles, observations and comments would be preserved for posterity as blueprints of the social structure we were building. It is certainly true of *Annabella Boswell's Journal*, which was originally published as a private edition more than a century ago under the title of *Early Reminiscences and Gleanings from an old Journal*.

Annabella's observations range over a wide area of the loosely knit settlements of New South Wales in the early 19th century but unquestionably, the most important part of the book is that dealing with Port Macquarie. Set largely in the gracious surroundings of the 'Lake Cottage', the home of her Uncle and Aunt, the Journal is written with all the freshness that a young woman can bring to record the day to day life of a microcosm of society that then existed in Australia and with the youthful unawareness of the problems then facing free settlers of Port Macquarie caught in the economic depression of that time.

Understandably, original works by early Colonial writers emerge slowly. In the case of *Early Reminiscences and Gleanings from an old Journal*, its survival after the private publication in Scotland by its authoress Annabella Boswell was almost accidental. How a copy of this publication came to be lodged with the Port Macquarie Branch of the then Bank of New South Wales has been lost to memory and record. When rediscovered it was acquired in 1956 by the Hastings District Historical Society who were instrumental in bringing it before a wider audience with its republication in Australia in 1965.

This find was to provide that Society with an important historical reference. It opened up an intensive field of research into the involvement of those mentioned by Annabella in the development of Port Macquarie during the formative days of free settlement that followed the closure of the Penal Station in 1830.

The Journal also produced a compulsive desire to clear the site of the Lake Cottage, a curiosity that revealed a ruin which stands monument to an ambitious entrepreneur who, ultimately, was shackled by economic bonds almost as painful and destructive as the metal chains of those who had helped him build it. The clearing disclosed evidence of the devastating bush fire of 1905 when this shingle-roofed mansion lay helplessly in its fiery path. There were also clear signs of the vandal, the pilferer and the souvenir hunter of the Innes-marked bricks.

Annabella's Journal was then to become the reference by which Richard Ratcliffe was to relate his Architectural drawing (see p. 000) of the ruined Georgian mansion to that which was once modestly referred to as the 'Lake Cottage'. It was later to encourage him during a brief visit to Britain to acquire for the Society the illustrations that appear in this edition.

The configuration of the Lake Cottage followed that of Northern Hemisphere homes rather than that now accepted in this part of the world. Its bedrooms faced the prevailing southerly winter winds and the living areas the receding sun. To it Innes brought his bride, Margaret, daughter of Colonial Secretary Alexander McLeay, and, within the eight years preceding Annabella's first visit to Lake Innes, Mrs Innes had transformed a part of this primitive area into a 'lovely garden'.

While, as Morton Herman mentions in his Introduction, there may well have been some ecological change at Lake Innes since 1826 when Annabella's Uncle was Commandant of the Port Macquarie Penal Station, it was obvious, as Innes's application for a Primary Grant was to prove, that he was aware of the primordial nature of this area of land. One can imagine that he saw in this place a reminder of 'Thrumster', his home in Caithness. Here were untouched lakes, reminders of the Locks of Yarehouse, Hempriggs and Sarclet so close to his old home. A home here would be no more isolated from the settlement of Port Macquarie than 'Thrumster' was from the Royal Burgh of Wick.

Annabella's marriage at the age of thirty to Patrick Boswell eventually led her and her four children back to this land of her forebears. There in the Boswell estate in Ayrshire they made their home at Garrallen, Old Cumnock, and in the surrounds of this manorial home there is still to this day evidence of the love of gardening developed at Lake Innes and reflected in its landscaping.

Sunday worship would have meant a pleasant carriage drive to Cumnock where the family were staunch supporters of the Church of Scotland. A plain memorial window with the Boswell Coat of Arms as its centrepiece still throws a warm bluish light on the gallery while the memorial wall plaques recognise these early colonists' service to the Church they had worshipped in since 1866.

It was an adventurous step by Angus & Robertson to re-publish in 1965 *Early Reminiscences and Gleanings from an old Journal* under a new title. It could hardly be considered the ideal time to introduce a new and unknown female writer to the reading public, particularly as her subject embraced Port Macquarie, a somewhat obscure North Coast town regarded more as a holiday spot than a place whose early history had somehow become lost along the way.

RONALD HOWELL

Hastings District
Historical Society,
1987

FOREWORD

INTRODUCTION

THIS JOURNAL is a record of the Australia of the 1830s and 1840s made by a girl and a woman, both the same person.
At that time Australia was a collection of loosely-knit settlements in New South Wales and Tasmania, with further embryo settlements in what were to become the States of Victoria, South Australia and Western Australia. Queensland had only a few outposts. Communication with the interior was by rough roads, but between points on the coast the most economical and natural means of transport was by ship. Sydney was beginning to think of itself as a city by 1840, with self-government in the air. Convict stations had been moved northwards, first to Newcastle, then to Port Macquarie, and later to Brisbane. But by 1840 the transportation of convicts to New South Wales ceased, although, of course, those convicts already here had to finish their sentences.
Australia was still a rough, harsh land but this present book is not a story of squalid frontier hardships, oppressed convicts and brutal bushrangers. All these do appear in the narrative, but only as incidents in, or as a backdrop to the main scenes in which there are great homesteads and mansions where their genteel occupants lived rich lives made easier by the presence of butlers and grooms, liveried footmen and personal maids.

It is a beautifully written book for it has all the freshness of the diary of a young girl, tempered and polished by the mature mind of the same girl grown to womanhood.

Annabella, whose maiden name was Innes, was born near Bathurst, New South Wales, in September 1826. When, some forty years later, she went with her husband to Scotland, her love of Australia went with her, eventually to show in almost every line of her book. She re-cast her diary in the form we see here. Sometimes she quotes her original girlish writings verbatim; sometimes they have obviously been altered and polished, since there is evident a much more mature judgment than would be found in a young girl's observations. At most times it will be clear to the reader which is the original diary and which the later commentary; but at times the two are inextricably entangled. Sometimes an overwhelming nostalgia gives a too-glamorous picture of the places so lovingly recollected. Annabella Boswell published several small books in Scotland, including the present Journal, before her death in 1916 at the age of ninety. All these were founded on her diary and other notes made so long before.

Annabella's early life was spent in a number of places, Bathurst and Sydney, Liverpool, Capertee, South Creek and Parramatta. She also visited widely about the colony of New South Wales. As this was during her childhood the recollections are less detailed than those of Port Macquarie which form the main interest of this book. However many of the places and buildings she mentions are still recognizable. To a small proportion of these, and to the names of a number of people, I have given footnotes in the text: others can readily be identified from historical sources.

It is the wealth of detail, the petty day-to-day things that Annabella records, that seem to bring alive the word-pictures she paints for us: glimpses of a Governor fixing a veil to his hat to keep at bay the ferocious flies of the Australian bush; the same Governor, "immensely tall and stout", at a ball; one of Nelson's tars off the *Victory* tending hens and hinting that he is out of "baccy"; an acquaintance going to India with horses, those Walers which were so long popular with the Indian Army; all these and hundreds of others give us bright flashes of the past.

Although recording the observations of a young girl, the diary perforce touches on major events such as the great economic depression of the early 1840s which had such an effect on the life of every colonial Australian. Not only womanly things engaged Annabella's attention: here and there we find a shrewd observation on the planning of a house or the clearing of bushland. A gentleman who demonstrated to her the cracking of a stockwhip was astonished when she took the whip and cracked it as well as he.

Her writings must have been voluminous. Her skill in English came from a succession of what must have been competent governesses. No matter how remote a house might be in those early days, the education of children was not neglected in important families.

The most important part of this book is unquestionably that dealing with Port Macquarie where, with her mother and sister, Annabella went to live in 1843. The trip from Sydney to Port Macquarie, it may be noted, was made by steamer and not by sailing ship, for steam came to the New South Wales coastal trade early in the 1830s. Her father, George Innes, having died, the family moved to Port Macquarie, taking their furniture with them with the idea of setting up house. However, Annabella's uncle, Major Innes, offered them a home at Lake Innes House just outside the town.

The remains of Lake Innes House are probably the only ones in all Australia that are identified on ordnance survey maps as "Ruins"—a most unlikely word to find in Australian cartography.

The whole district around the house is ruined, or, perhaps it would be better to say, has relapsed into its former primitive state. To fly over Lake Innes is to see a sheet of water surrounded by primordial swamp into the fringes of which settlement has not even penetrated. To enter the forest of Lake

Innes House it to realize that nature has entirely and heartlessly reclaimed all the area so lovingly depicted in Annabella Boswell's book. The present wild desolation seems to bear no resemblance to the former scenes she so vividly described.

There is a trick of cinematography often used to amuse news-reel addicts whereby an event like an explosion demolishing a whole hillside is run backwards through the projector so that all the fallen rubble and debris seems to leap backward to replace the hillside in its former condition. To go over the ground of Lake Innes House and then read Annabella Boswell is to experience much the same feeling. The desolation and forest lands seem to disappear and once more we see the broad clearings, flower gardens and lawns of yesteryear. By the devoted and intricate archaeological researches of Richard Ratcliffe and his helpers we are even able to see Lake Innes House. The illustrations reproduced elsewhere in this book show it as it was, a large, rambling, pleasant Georgian house that Major Innes very modestly referred to as the Lake Cottage. The multiplicity of outbuildings made the isolated domestic establishment almost completely self-supporting. Nowadays all that can be distinguished on the site is a scrap of wall here and there, and an odd chimney or two thrusting up above the twenty-foot high surf of Mysore Thorn that has all but engulfed the lonely shreds of brickwork that represent a once-great house. When in a small patch of jungle the northern steps of the erstwhile veranda are found, the tree growing out of them seems to increase the desolation.

The bamboos mentioned in the diary are still there clacking forlornly in the wind, and the thorn and lantana which Major Innes imported to make the pretty hedges and arches so beloved of Annabella have spread across the landscape so far that they are referred to locally as the Innes Curse. The Moreton Bay chestnut-tree mentioned in the diary still flowers in the spring.

With fine farming and dairy country all around it is difficult to imagine why Major Innes chose the site he did for his house. It is on the end of a low spur that runs through heavy forest surrounded on three sides by some of the dreariest jungle swamp imaginable. Admittedly it is evident from Annabella's writings that he cleared openings in the forest which would have given the house some breathing space, and would have moved to some distance from it all the loathsome insects and reptiles which infest the forest.

Annabella does mention a plague of mosquitoes on the occasion of a vice-regal visit to the house. The plague is still there, but so are other things of which curiously no mention is made in her text. Standing in the forest today viewing the ruins of the house one is not only driven almost to distraction by clouds of mosquitoes, but a wary eye has to be kept on the ground if it is the least moist to be able to avoid the hordes of leeches writhing forward to suck unwary blood. The bark of trees, too, conceals ugly ticks ready to drop on one for the same purpose, and care must be taken when thrusting through the undergrowth that snakes are not disturbed into belligerence.

This is an awesome contrast to that lovely day in January 1843 when Annabella in approaching the house "walked up the wide approach . . . the air cool and fresh, laden with the sweet scent of roses and heliotrope, the leaves of the evergreens glittering in the sun, and a thousand gay flowers lending brightness to the scene". At the foot of sloping ground to the right lay Lake Innes, shining in the sun. No water can now be seen from that position since an almost impenetrable jungle of swampy growth shuts off the lake upon which she gazed with such admiration, and upon which she was subsequently to take such delightful boating trips. Today the lake is all but stranger to man: the only ones that visit it at long intervals are fishermen from Port Macquarie who, with the instinct of their trade, know when the lake mullet are ready for harvesting. At such periods a boat is brought overland from Port Macquarie, taken along a ricketty catwalk specially built through the swamp, and finally launched on the waters of the lake. Possibly Annabella saw the lake with a higher level than at present. The building of a drain at the southernmost end may have lowered the water level and so caused an even greater area of lake-surrounding swamp than existed in her day.

Of the clearings she mentions, virtually nothing now remains. The forest has not only closed in upon the house, but has invaded it; great trees grow in what were formerly the rooms in which she describes such gay events taking place. The areas formerly occupied by orchards and garden can just be discerned by a slight lightening of the density of the forest as it sweeps down to the lake, but the difference is not enough to influence the statement that nature has regained all that Major Innes wrested from it. The whole area is now as if no settlement had ever been there. Access to the house ruins is by what was once the estate road, now degenerated into a track through the forest. Here and there, if one explores, hidden from all but those who seek them out, can be found open-cut red oxide mines whose blood-red gashes in the soil of the forest are surprising flashes of vivid colour.

Major Archibald C. Innes was an important man in Australian history. He was twenty-three years old when he left England as an army captain in charge of convicts. After three years in Tasmania he was ordered to Port Macquarie as Commandant; which post he held only briefly, for in 1827 he was Police Magistrate at Parramatta. In 1829 he married Margaret, third daughter of the Colonial Secretary, Alexander Macleay. He resigned his position at Parramatta and returned to Port Macquarie as a settler, having in the meantime secured fat government contracts for the supply of primary produce.

He had a grant of 2,650 acres at Lake Burrawan, which he promptly re-named Lake Innes. Clearing of the ground and the building of Lake Innes House began straight away, and the Major secured other large properties in the New England district, and on the Darling River. He built a road from Port Macquarie to the inland and, having ready access to large quantities of convict labour, he was lavish in all his enterprises, which prospered for a number of years. His hospitality at Lake Innes House, too, was lavish and it was his amiable habit to offer, free of charge, the use of a horse to any army officer stationed at the Port.

His prosperity began to wane after the transportation of convicts to New South Wales ceased in 1840, but he was still able to entertain the Governor, Sir Charles Fitz Roy, at the house with great ceremony in 1847. Annabella's recollections of this period are fascinating. Ten years later the Major's fortune had all but disappeared and he accepted the position of Police Magistrate in the Newcastle District. He died in Newcastle in 1857 and is buried in the grounds of Christ Church Cathedral. His house at Port Macquarie was occupied by a succession of people for a time, but it gradually decayed, and was finally destroyed by a bushfire which raged through the forest which was already beginning to reclaim the clearings that the Major had made.

The Port Macquarie that Annabella knew also has disappeared, to be replaced by the present architecturally unexciting pleasure resort. The only significant building remaining from her time is St Thomas's Church, which, although she never mentions it by name, is the one at which she worshipped and at times held Sunday-school. Built in 1826 when Port Macquarie was at its height as a convict settlement, St Thomas's was the northernmost church in Australia until the building in 1856 of the first Christ Church (on the site of the present cathedral) in Grafton on the Clarence River. St Thomas's remains today, with St John's, Stroud, as one of the two virtually unspoilt early colonial churches on the whole mainland of Australia.

The local Council and the local Historical Society in the interests of history have caused notices to be put throughout Port Macquarie indicating the sites of early buildings that used to stand there—which is something; but not as good as having the buildings themselves. Many of the Port's minor but architecturally valuable buildings have been lost only recently. The heavy tourist traffic to St Thomas's church shows just how deep is Australia's interest in its past now that it is almost too late to see any of it.

Outside the town many of the geographical features men-tioned by Annabella are easily recognized. Tacking Point, round which she used so often to watch vessels sailing, Cathie Creek, Blackman's Point and all the rest of them are there, just as she described. Although the man-made world she frequented at or near Port Macquarie has all but disappeared, Annabella's writings bring back a locality, a house, an era, with such vivid-ness that we can enjoy an Australia that once was, almost as though we were her contemporaries.

MORTON HERMAN

1967

PUBLISHER'S NOTE

PATRICK CHARLES DOUGLAS-BOSWELL, Annabella's husband, was descended from the same ancestral stock as the immortal James Boswell. The publishers are indebted to Professor Frederick A. Pottle, chairman of the editorial committee of the Yale editions of the private papers of James Boswell, for information as to the family relationship, and to Mrs Pottle for the following summary:

> Annabella (Innes) Boswell's husband, Patrick Charles Douglas-Boswell of Garrallan, was a descendant of John Boswell, 3rd Laird of Auchinleck (d. about 1609). This John Boswell of Auchinleck had 3 sons:
>
> 1. James, 4th Laird of Auchinleck, ancestor of James Boswell, the biographer.
> 2. John, of Duncanziemore, founder of the Craigston Boswells.
> 3. William, of Knockroon, founder of the Knockroon family.
>
> The Craigston Boswells and the Boswells of Knockroon intermarried and their descendants are the Douglas-Boswells of Garrallan, and of Auchinleck.
>
> It will be seen that the relationship is remote so far as the generations are concerned. James Boswell, the biographer, however, had a strong sense of kinship with John Boswell, the laird of Knockroon of his day, grandfather of Patrick Charles Douglas-Boswell.
>
> A chart showing the connections of the Boswells may be found on p. 375 of *Boswell: The Ominous Years, 1774-1776*, edited by Charles Ryskamp and Frederick A. Pottle (McGraw-Hill Book Co., N.Y., William Heinemann, London, 1963).

Patrick was born in Ayrshire, Scotland, in 1816, the son of Jane Douglas and Hamilton Douglas-Boswell. He emigrated to Australia and became a settler on the Lachlan River. In 1853 (according to information supplied by Miss Patricia Quinn, archivist of the Bank of New South Wales, Sydney) he was appointed "acting receiving teller" at the bank's Newcastle (New South Wales) branch, afterwards being promoted to accountant and, in 1858, manager. He also held shares in the bank. He married Annabella Innes at Christchurch Cathedral, Newcastle, on 17th June, 1856. In 1864 he applied for twelve months' leave of absence from the bank to visit England, and in 1866, from Garrallan, Cumnock, Scotland, he wrote to Sydney resigning his position for the reason that "I find that at any rate for the next two years it is really necessary I should be handy to watch the development of certain matters that may turn out of much importance to me." The "certain matters" were connected with the inheritance of family estates.

Annabella Boswell's Journal, as her book is here entitled, was originally published, largely for the information of the author's children, under the title *Early Recollections and Gleanings, from an Old Journal.* In order to take the modern reader swiftly into the direct movement of the story, which really begins in 1834 when Annabella finds herself at school in Bridge Street, Sydney, and proceeds to relate her own experiences in chronological order, the text of the original first few pages has been re-arranged in the present edition; while some appendixes which gave an impression of anticlimax have been omitted.

Parts of the original opening pages relating to Annabella's ancestors, and her earliest childhood memories, which, though interesting in themselves, impeded the flow of the narrative, have been re-assembled in Appendix 1. From the sentence beginning "Early in 1834" (p. 3), until the conclusion "I revisited it once only, five years afterwards" (p. 167), the text, with a few minor typographical changes, is identical with the original. Annabella's variations in spellings of proper names and place-names have, in general, been retained. Where possible, the distinction between her original diary and her later interpolations has been indicated by spaces on the page. The Journal is here reprinted by courtesy of Mrs Patricia Douglas-Boswell, Auchinleck.

Grateful acknowledgment for help in research is made to the Librarian and staff of the Mitchell Library, Sydney, particularly Miss Mourot and Miss M. K. Beddie; and to Mr K. Gollan of the Hastings District Historical Society, Port Macquarie.

Richard Ratcliffe of Newcastle, New South Wales, collated much information about Lake Innes House, and did the preliminary work that led to the re-publication of the Journal. His reconstruction drawings of Lake Innes House, and an account of his researches, are included in this edition.

CONTENTS

Chapter

1

TO SCHOOL
IN BRIDGE STREET

I WAS BORN at Yarrows, near Bathurst in New South Wales, in 1826, in September, which in that favoured land is a sweet spring month, when all nature is fresh and gay. The sombre green of the trees, which never shed their leaves, is then relieved by wild flowers of every size and hue, from the gaudy waratah to the lovely fringed violet, and every garden is gay with flowers and blossoms.

We left Yarrows while I was still an infant, and I never saw the place again. The house was situated on Winburndale Creek, where also my father had built a mill, but I suppose it did not thrive, as our next home was for a time at his cattle station in a very inaccessible place called Capita, or Capertee, about sixty miles from Bathurst.

Before entering on my own recollections, I must say something of what I have heard from my parents, and give a few particulars of their respective families.

My parents were married in St John's Church, Parramatta,[1] on 25th November 1825. Miss E. Macarthur, of Elizabeth Farm,[2] was one of the bridesmaids, my aunt Isabella the other. My

[1] Only the towers remain of the church of Annabella's time.
[2] Although much altered, Elizabeth Farm is the oldest existing building in Australasia.

mother was just twenty, my father two or three years older.
A handsome young couple they were, and began life with
every prospect of success. My Innes relations seem to have
smiled on this early marriage and to have loaded the young
people with gifts. I remember a huge wooden chest, which
we as children used to regard with much interest, as having
been sent from home, full of good gifts to our parents.

My father, George Innes, was the eighth son of Major James
Innes, of Thrumster, Caithness, and Margaret Clunes, and was
born in 1803. If so, he was just twenty years old when in 1823
he sailed for Sydney, N.S.W., a passenger in a ship of which
his brother, Captain Archibald Clunes Innes, 3rd Buffs, was
Captain of the guard of soldiers in charge of the convicts
who formed the unhappy freight. I am not sure of the name
of the ship, but think it was the *Eliza,* nor do I know any
particulars of the voyage. I have often wondered how my
grandmother consented to let her son go out so young and
almost alone to such banishment, for my uncle fully expected
to go on at once to India. As it happened, he never went; he
was appointed to some arduous duties in Van Diemen's Land
(now Tasmania) and two years afterwards he nearly died from
an illness brought on by over-fatigue and exposure while there.
Meantime my father had taken up a grant of land at Winburndale Creek, near Bathurst, and had there built a cottage and
a mill. He had also established an out station for cattle at
Umbiella, Capita [Capertee].

My grandfather Campbell's family came originally from
Perthshire, and were a branch of the Bredalbane Campbells.
He married about 1800 Annabella, daughter of Col. John
Campbell of Melfort. They went to live in Kingsborough House,
in the Isle of Skye, where their numerous family was born.
They remained there till about 1816, and moved then to Lochend
[near Appin, Argyllshire] on the death of his father. Eight
sons and five daughters were alive when, in 1821, they
determined to emigrate to Australia, encouraged in the idea
by the Governor at that time who was a friend and relation

of my grandfather, General Lachlan M'quarrie. I have often listened with delight to my mother's description of her early days at Kingsborough, though inwardly rejoicing that she did not exercise towards us the same rigid discipline that her mother saw fit to adopt towards her children. My grandfather was a warm admirer of Prince Charles Edward and, living in Kingsborough House, which had once sheltered him, gave a reality to the tales they heard about him, and impressed them deeply on the minds of the elder children.

Early in 1834 I found myself settled at school in Bridge Street, Sydney, under the care of Mrs Evans, and her friend and partner, Miss Ferris. Mr Evans had a large bookseller's and stationer's shop, and we occupied the rest of the house, which at that time was thought handsome, and in a fashionable street. Our house faced the old Government Stores or Depôt,[1] and close by flowed the Tank Stream, now arched over and made into the main drain of that portion of the populous city.

We were quite near the old Government House[2] and Macquarie Place, where lived the leading Government Officials: these houses were back from the street, and had pretty gardens and deep verandas, sheltered by climbing roses, and other flowering plants. I do not remember that I ever was in the old Government House, but I made many happy visits to our kind friends Mr and Mrs Macleay at Macquarie Place.[3] He was then, and for many years, Colonial Secretary: one of his daughters had married my uncle, Major Innes. They were then living at Lake Innes, Port Macquarie. Miss Macleay, afterwards Mrs Harrington, was very kind to me. I have since heard that she wished to adopt and educate me herself. She died in 1836, only a few weeks after her marriage. Miss Kennethena Macleay (dear kind Aunt Kenny) was also very good to me. I remember sitting on

[1] It was known as the Lumber Yard and was on the south side of Bridge Street between George and Pitt Streets.
[2] This was the first Government House, started in 1788. It was superseded by the present Government House in 1845.
[3] Their house was designed by architect D. D. Mathew, and it lasted until 1914.

the floor in her room and watching with the liveliest interest while her hair was being dressed in the fashion of that day: at the back a wonderful erection, supported by a high backed tortoise-shell comb, and in front curls. Her hair was very red, and she was not pretty, but I admired her very much.

My parents went to Capita after leaving me at school, so when Easter came I could not go home for the holidays, and had a very vague idea as to what would become of me when everyone else went home. Nothing happened as was expected. Very wet weather came on, the Tank Stream overflowed its banks and rushed into the basement of our house. Late one Saturday night an alarm was raised that the foundations were giving way. Many houses were flooded, and people were being taken out of the water.

I really do not know if we were in any danger, but a party of soldiers came to our rescue. No doubt it was great fun for some of the young officers, and I know that some of the girls enjoyed it too, and were delighted to be carried off in their strong arms to a place of safety. I was a miserable little urchin, but of course, I had to be rescued too. I was one of four who were most kindly received by Mr and Mrs W. H. McKenzie, of the Bank of Australasia. She was a Miss Hawkins, a friend of my mother's. The rain continued to fall in torrents, the old guard house was swept away, part of the barrack wall[1] came down, and damage was done everywhere. It was a terrible Easter Sunday for many, but we were comfortably housed, and next day I was sent for by Mrs Macleay, and spent in her house one of the happiest times of my young life: all were so kind and clever, and all their surroundings were so refined and luxurious in comparison to anything I, who had lived mostly in the bush, was accustomed to.

There was a grand dinner party given during one of my visits at Macquarie Place. I was deeply interested in watching some of the preparations for it, and still remember the lovely fruit and flowers, though they were not used in the same way then

[1] In Wynyard Square.

"Early in 1834 I found
myself settled at school in Sydney."

TO SCHOOL IN BRIDGE STREET

8

as now, to decorate the dinner table. I saw pomegranates then for the first time; when freshly gathered and very ripe they are very different from the withered balls generally seen in this country. Dessert was laid out on the library table ready to be taken to the dining-room after dinner and placed on the shining board after the tablecloth had been removed, as was the custom then and long after. I had dined daintily in the library, and after dinner I was sent for by the kind old gentleman, and, standing beside him, shared the feast.

In the drawing-room I was much noticed by Mrs Sturt, afterwards Lady Sturt, wife of Captain Charles Sturt, who was then absent with an exploring party near the Murrumbidgee River. There was much interesting conversation on the subject, all the more interesting to those present as one of Mr Macleay's sons was with Captain Sturt. I enjoyed more than anything the drives to Elizabeth Bay, a lovely spot beyond Woolloomooloo, where Mr Macleay was then laying out fine gardens and grounds, and preparing to build a large and handsome house. When completed it was for many years quite the finest house[1] in the colony, and must always remain one of the loveliest situations. There I used to play while the elders of the party were occupied about the grounds, and the time passed all too quickly.

During the Easter holidays Mrs Evans moved from the house in Bridge Street, and when the school reassembled we found ourselves in a large and convenient detached house standing in its own grounds. Albion House, Miller Point, Darling Harbour, was the address. No doubt the place has changed long ago beyond my recognition. I have never seen it since I left it for good the following year. I was not happy there. I still had my playfellows, Anna Cox and Mrs Evans's eldest girl. Mr Evans had been married before, and a daughter of his, about sixteen, was one of the elder girls. She was always gentle and good to the little ones, but the school increased greatly, and there were too many big girls, some vulgar and disagreeable.

[1] Elizabeth Bay House designed by John Verge. It still exists.

8

Such a mixture was a great mistake; they persecuted the little ones, and one very bad thing was their continual telling of ghost stories and murders, and declaring that the house was haunted. Then when all were trembling with fear and excitement someone was dared to go upstairs, or one of the little ones was sent a message and made to go alone. I professed to have no fear, but I had a severe illness in that house and thought I saw a ghost in my bedroom, and wonder now that it did not more seriously affect me. I told Mrs Evans all about it, and she saw how foolishly and thoughtlessly the girls had behaved, and put a stop to it.

There was a horrid girl there who used to slap me. One day I struck her in return, and we had a regular fight. I never had been in a passion before and never have been since; murder was in my heart, fury in my eyes. I was only eight; she was twelve or fourteen, but I was victorious, and thoroughly ashamed of myself for long afterwards. One girl only of my schoolfellows I met in after years; her family had a sad history. Another that I liked very much, and who was nearer my own age, was drowned in a ship lost at sea—no tidings ever came of any of those who were on board.

I had been at school more than a year when one joyful day my father arrived to take me home for good. How gladly I turned my back on that page of my life. I was a very tall girl, nearer nine than eight years old, and felt very important during our journey home, while I occupied the seat beside him in his neat gig, and chatted gaily of many things. We were all to go shortly to Bathurst to stay with our good friends, the George Rankens,[1] at Saltram, a place recently bought by him from Mr T. Icely,[2] and on which stood a house much larger than that at Kiloshiel. But first I must tell of our safe arrival at home and the warm welcome I there received from my dear mother and charming little sister. My happiness was complete. I had been at Glen Alice before, but not since the house was begun.

[1] George Ranken became a magistrate.
[2] Thomas Icely was an important merchant.

TO SCHOOL IN BRIDGE STREET

I found it still unfinished, but very comfortable, and the garden beautifully laid out and well stocked with vines and fruit trees. It was then mid-winter.

On the 26th July we started for Bathurst. Our first stage was twenty-five miles to Cullenbullen, where we were most kindly received by Mrs Dalhunty, her grown-up daughter, and her son, Dr Dalhunty, very nice English people, and their house a picture of English neatness and comfort. We rested there a night, and next night we were to stop at the Green Swamp, at an inn about fifteen miles from Bathurst. The weather was very cold and damp. We two children were in the gig with our father, mamma rode near us on her pretty cream coloured mare Rowena, and the groom, George F. M., rode behind.

A blinding shower of sleet came on, our horse shied, and the wheel of the gig came in contact with a fallen tree—the gig upset, I somehow fell under it, the others were thrown out. My first recollection on awakening was to find my face cut and bleeding, and my mother trying to discover if any of my bones were broken. The groom had been sent off to the inn to beg them to send a conveyance for us, while he went on to Bathurst for the doctor. It was late in the evening when Dr Busby arrived, and by that time we had all cheered up. He found I was not badly hurt, a deep cut on my forehead, which left an ugly scar, and some scratches and bruises, which soon disappeared, being all the damage. Uncle Dalmahoy came out from Bathurst with the doctor, and it being Mag's birthday, and as a reward for my bravery after the accident, he was good enough to present us each with a half-sovereign, a gift treasured for years, and finally spent in the purchase of two tiny gold lockets. He was our favourite uncle, not because of his gifts, but because he loved us.

We spent three months at Saltram at this time. My father went to Yass to purchase sheep for his station near Capita, called, I think, Boorroobin. One day the gentlemen returned from the Settlement bringing the good news that Major Mitchell, the Surveyor General and party had returned safely from an exploring expedition into the far bush. There was great rejoicing and excitement throughout the colony, as the explorers had discovered a fine pastoral country to the south-east. People talked of at once taking up and stocking the new country, part of which was named Australia Felix. It is now absorbed into Victoria.

Mrs Ranken's family then consisted of four boys and four girls. The two eldest boys were at school, or just going: they still had their former tutor, Mr Darney, and the girls had a charming governess, an old friend and companion of their mother, who had come from Scotland to live with her, and to help her with her numerous family, and the duties and pleasures of a large establishment. Aunt Annabella was staying at Saltram, also Isabella Johnstone, and a delightful family lately come from Scotland lived at Delta Cottage and were constantly there. It was a large and merry household. In September Mrs Ranken gave a dance.

I can remember many of the guests and their dresses, and how we children criticized them. There was a pretty Miss Brooks, with long fair hair. I saw her many years afterwards as Mrs Zouch, and a grandmother. There were two Misses Stewart and two Misses Piper, and Miss De Philipsthal. The latter wore a short yellow dress and black shoes with sandals, her hair dressed high with bunches of curls at each side. Miss Geddis, Ann Macarthur, and many others were present. Aunt Anna, I suppose, was really the belle, and the dance was given partly in her honour, as she was going to Sydney to stay with her eldest sister, Mrs McLeod. Mr McLeod had for some time held a Government appointment in Norfolk Island, but it was far from being a desirable place of residence, and he had just returned to Sydney with his family. This lovely island was then a Penal Settlement, a place of punishment for the worst class of criminals, and a station for a strong body of soldiers who kept guard over them. Mr McLeod was wise to leave. He then settled for a time at a place called Maryvale, near Liverpool, where we visited them in 1839.

But to return to Saltram. We stayed there till October 1835, and soon after our return home we were happy in being put under the care of an excellent governess. Her name was Miss Willis, and I am sure no children ever had a kinder or more painstaking teacher. My mother, too, found her helpful in many ways, and an acquisition in our isolated home. We children threw ourselves with zeal into our work. I panted for information, and read greedily every book I was allowed to have. We read many times the histories of England, Scotland, Greece, and Rome. The story of *Elizabeth, or the Exiles of Siberia* was an especial favourite, and we had many other nice books, considering the time and the place.

Miss Willis had a guitar; she was not very proficient, but she taught us to play nicely and to sing some simple songs. For grammar she had a mania. I think I learned every word of a large Murray by heart; her zeal never flagged. We played at spelling lessons; the spelling Bees of recent years would, I am sure, have been a joy to her. One of our amusements was that we each wrote a letter every week. I have a few of these compositions beside me now; many were to imaginary people. Those we really wrote and sent had also to be copied into the letter-book. In those days of exorbitant postage very few went beyond it. I have seen a letter for which seven and eightpence postage was paid. I shall give an example of one of the letters that was sent. It is number fourteen, dated 16th April 1836, and was addressed to my uncle, Major Innes, Lake Innes, Port Macquarie:

> It gives me very great pleasure to write to you, my dear uncle, and papa tells me I must send you the little drawing I have just finished this afternoon. Had I known it was to be sent to you I would have taken more pains with it.
>
> We have got a governess now. I like it much better than being at school, because I do not require to leave dear papa and mamma. I am learning to play the guitar; I found it very difficult at first. I made my fingers so sore and my arms ache, but now my fingers have got quite hard at the points, and I am getting on very well with it. I can play the accompaniment to "Ye Banks

and Braes" and to "Ah Vousdirais", "Rondo", and a few other little airs. I am reading the history of England, and have got the length of James the First, who began the reign of the family of the Stuart's in England. I like my studies very much indeed; they are a pleasure to me. Miss Willis explains them as I go on, which makes them easy to be understood. I think I like geography better than any of my other lessons. I have gone through the four quarters of the globe with Miss Willis, and I begin again on Monday at the map of Europe and through each country, beginning at England. My sister gets on very well with her lessons. She writes very well indeed, and seems to have a great taste for drawing. She is also learning to play the guitar. I wrote to Grandmamma in December, and since then I have written to aunt Jane. They cannot have got my letters yet, and very much pleased I shall be if my aunt writes to me. I intend to write to one of my aunts soon. I hope my dear little cousins are well. I suppose Gordina begins to run about now. Papa, Mamma, and Margaret join me in sending their love to you and my aunt, and kisses to my dear cousins. Goodbye, my dear uncle.—Believe me, etc.

A. A. C. INNES.

The next letter is to my aunt Annabella, then staying with her sister, Mrs M'Leod, in Sydney:

Glen Alice, Capita, May 17th, 1836.

My Dear Aunt,

I am quite glad to have an opportunity of writing to you. I fancy I have got so much to communicate that I scarcely know which subject to commence first. I received your nice letter when the drays came back from Sydney. I assure you I was very proud of it, and Maggie thought herself quite a big lady because she had got a letter from you. She kissed it over and over again, and went about showing it to every one.

I am making a basket of cardboard, which I intend to present to Mr Ranken; it is nearly finished. I have painted an Indian tare on the one side, and that pretty blue flower called native flax on the other. On one end I have put a little purple aster and on the other I have sketched the Deil in the Bush, which I intend to paint. I think it will look very pretty. Miss Willis paints all the native flowers we can find for copies for us. If I have time I shall endeavour to take one from nature to send to you. I am getting on very well with the guitar, and can play several long pieces, besides three pretty waltzes and the accompaniments for three songs. I assure you I never look off the book now when I am playing. Miss Willis had a great deal of trouble with me at first. I am so glad I can do it now.

I write a long letter every week; it is sometimes three pages and sometimes four. I wish you were here to read them; I think they would amuse you, there is something about you in almost every one of them. In the one for this week I have you lost in the bush with Margaret, Miss Willis and me, at Hunter's River, where we are supposed to be on a visit to Aunt Ogilvie, after having spent a month in Sydney with Aunt McLeod. I have written to her after going to Hunter's river; the letter this week is in answer to one I imagined Nancy to have written to me.

Margaret is a very good girl, she improves in reading, and indeed in all her lessons; you cannot think how well she says her notes. She made us laugh today when we were sitting drawing. Miss Willis told her to take pains and draw nicely, for it was to be sent to her aunt, and she answered—"You may think what pains I am taking, for my arm is pains all over."

Mamma is very busy getting trees planted out. She hopes you do not forget to collect all the seeds you can find for her. Our garden looks very well at present. There has been a great deal of rain. We have plenty of green peas, and all kinds of vegetables. The fowls are not laying, so I am very little use as a hen-wife. All here join in kind love to you, and I remain my dear Aunt, Your most affectionate niece.

Just one other short letter I must give, written to my father at Cullen Bullen:

June 29th, 1836.

My Dear Papa,

Mamma is very anxious to get some cuttings of the Cluster Rose or Honeysuckle, and any other pretty thing you can find in Mr Dalhunty's garden. We have sent several times for some, but have not been able to get any to grow: this is such a delightful season, Mamma thinks they would be sure to grow now. We went to the Creek about a fortnight ago, and got a great many beautiful shrubs and runners, and we have made the place look so pretty. We are all quite impatient for your return, so do make haste and come. Mamma is quite well, and unites with Margaret and me in sending you a thousand kisses. Believe me, dear Papa, your most affectionate daughter A. A. C. Innes.

Observe the confidence with which we claim a share of our neighbour's most cherished possessions, but I must add that we were always ready and willing to give anything in return. It was a mutual pleasure to give and receive seeds and plants, and my dear mother delighted in her garden. I quite well remember our expedition to the Creek, alluded to in my letter to my father. It was a lovely sheltered stream, flowing from one of the many hills which surrounded our happy valley. After rains it ran rapidly, forming many little sparkling falls, and filling deep water holes bordered with flowering shrubs and creepers, but only as far as it was under the shade and shelter of the hill.

High up, these hills had a rocky crown up which we never penetrated, but we scrambled along the banks of more than one ravine, and found many lovely wild flowers. I have drawings of many of them, and we from time to time transplanted many varieties of them to our garden and shrubbery: some were flourishing when in 1841 we left Glen Alice for good. We really had a beautiful garden in front of the house, but not too near, and the ground between was prettily laid out with lawn and shrubbery, all planned by Mr John Maclean, at one time head gardener in the Botanical Gardens, Sydney, and afterwards holding a government appointment at Norfolk Island, where unfortunately he was drowned.

In 1836 we had a very happy Christmas. Our uncles came over from Warrangee, and Mr Andrew Brown, and Mr David Archer from Wallerowang. We dined for the first time in the large central room of the house, though it was not yet plastered. We were allowed to adorn the lathed walls with evergreens and flowers, which looked bright and pretty. Our house was comfortable, but by no means commodious, even after the dining-room was finished. There were only five rooms, a wide back entrance, and a deep veranda in front. We sat a good deal in the veranda, which was sheltered by many lovely creepers.

Early in 1837 we went to stay at the White Rock, near Bathurst, to be present at the marriage of my aunt, Annabella

Campbell, to Mr Arthur Ranken, which took place on 7th March. This was the first marriage at which I was present. It took place, of course, in the house. The Rev. K. Smythe performed the ceremony. Isabella Johnstone and Ann M'Arthur were bridesmaids. I do not remember who was best man. The bride was dressed in a rich white silk dress, the skirt rather short and full, low bodice, and bell-shaped sleeves.

Her hair, which was dark and very abundant, was dressed very high on the top of her head, and supported by a high-backed tortoise-shell comb, short curls in front, a tulle veil falling gracefully over her shoulders. The bridesmaids were both tall, and had their hair dressed in much the same style. The bridegroom wore white trousers and vest, and a dress coat of blue cloth, with brass buttons and lined with white silk. The happy pair went to Glen Alice for their honeymoon. We followed in about a fortnight. This was our first visit to the White

*"We scrambled along the banks
of more than one ravine."*

TO SCHOOL IN BRIDGE STREET

Rock. We also stayed a week or two with our kind friends at Saltram, but I cannot remember if it was in that or the following year they were preparing to go to Scotland.

When once settled at home we resumed our lessons with renewed vigour. Towards the end of the year, to our great regret, Miss Willis expressed her wish to leave. She said she was desirous of taking lessons in music and drawing, and finally she took a situation in a large school in Sydney. We had visions of her returning to us at some not distant period, but to our surprise she married a Wesleyan minister, a widower, with several children, and no doubt made an excellent wife and step-mother. She was so full of sentiment and of a romantic love story of her early life that this seemed a very commonplace conclusion to come to.

After Christmas we looked forward with anxious interest to the arrival of our new governess. Papa was to bring her from Sydney, and at the same time my eldest cousin, Annabella Macleod, to visit us and other friends at Bathurst; also, to our great delight, another cousin of our own age, Williamina Macleod, who was to share our studies under this new governess. Our castles in the air in this particular soon collapsed. A young lady appeared who I recognized at once as the girl who mended our clothes and taught us plain sewing at Mrs Evans's school— a sort of help, and quite unfit to be a governess. She excused herself by saying she expected to find us little children requiring only a nursery governess. It was very annoying, but she was only too glad to leave at once.

We went to the White Rock, Bathurst, again in March 1838, and stayed there three or four months. Our journey there is one of the first I remember of our numerous expeditions round The Peak, as the road which led to and from Capita was then called. Nothing could be worse than this road. We always had to sleep one or two nights in the bush, if anything more than one gig and one or two horsemen were of the party, as it took three men to help and encourage one good horse up and down these hills. On this occasion we were a large party. Uncle

Dalmahoy Campbell and Mr Jones had come to our assistance; each of them had a gig, and we had one too, also a dray, with a tent, bedding, and various supplies, to enable us to camp out for one or two nights. It was really very enjoyable, and we made light of any small inconveniences. We did not stay a night at Cullen Bullen, as we were so large a party, but we had dinner or tea there, and I was much impressed by Miss Dalhunty's appearance and with the very pretty house and Garden.

Arrived at the White Rock we found the house full to over-flowing. It is a mystery to me now how we were all stowed away. The place took its name from a quantity of beautiful white quartz which cropped up in the green grass, not far from the house. At that time no one associated quartz with gold, and no thought of the future wealth of the gold diggings, afterwards to be opened up in the Bathurst district, had dawned on anyone's mind. When we were staying there the year before, it was uncle Dalmahoy's house. He gave it up when aunt Anna married, and my youngest uncle (Moore) having lately married, **he and his wife were** living there. She was a Miss De Lisle, only child of Major De Lisle of the 80th regiment, a very kind and amiable girl, but at that time quite unfitted for the life she had, I think rather unwisely stepped into.

The house was built on the bare hillside and quite unimproved around. The River Macquarie flowed not far off to the right as one looked from the veranda, to the left lay the road to Bathurst, which was about four miles distant. We seldom went to the Settlement, as it was then generally called, but we spent many hours by the river fishing or watching for a platypus to appear, or lying under the great bluegum-trees, gathering manna. At the back of the house, some distance off, lay Queen Charlotte's vale. There were some pretty homesteads there, surrounded by cultivated fields, and standing mostly in gardens gay with flowers. On 31st March aunt Anna's eldest boy was born. He was a great joy and interest to us all till they left for their own home at Glen Logan, Lachlan River.

I remember, with pleasure, a visit I paid at this time to Mrs William Lawson at Macquarie Plains. She was a Miss Icely, a friend of my mother. No one could be kinder than she always was, and I enjoyed myself extremely. She then had four children, all younger than I was. It was a pleasant walk from there to Woodlands, the home of their nearest neighbours, Mr and Mrs Street, whose children were more my own age. Another event of interest was the marriage of Miss Anne Hawkins to Mr F. MacArthur. Two dances were given in honour of the happy occasion; to the second of these, given by Mrs Evernden (a sister of the bride), four little girls were invited, ladies being scarce. I was much delighted at being one of the number, though too shy to show my pleasure by dancing. I wore a white silk dress with pale blue sprigs on it. Andrewina Piper and Julia Bowler were quite at home and danced all the evening. The bride was tall and handsome, and a great favourite with everyone. I never saw her again, as she went with her husband to Yass. Years afterwards a daughter of theirs married a son of our friends, Mr and Mrs George Ranken, of Saltram.

In June Aunt Fanny had a little son. It was mid-winter and very cold, and I had dreadful chilblains. We were all glad to find ourselves at home again. We now had a new governess, Miss Smith by name, young and trained to be a governess, full of theories, and of her own importance, but we got on very well with her. She gave us plenty of work to do, and had no peace of mind till we had learned by rote the whole of Magnell's questions, and could say "King's Reign", with dates, without a mistake. At this time we got a piano. A most laborious business it was conveying it round The Peak, and scarcely worth the trouble.

Papa bought us also a pretty guitar, but Miss Smith despised it, as she also did our efforts at drawing from nature. She gave us stiff designs to copy, taught us to shade finely with pencil and to draw from copies, trees rare and wonderful, while our much-loved wild flowers were left unnoticed and our paint boxes set aside. During this summer our dear father was not at all well. He had been in Sydney for change of air most of the time that we spent at the White Rock, so as to avoid the sharp cold of Bathurst and Capita, but had not derived any permanent benefit from it.

A curious incident happened during our visit to the White Rock. The household was rather oddly constituted. We had a maidservant with us (a prisoner, as all servants, male and female, then were) and there was in the house a very smart English housemaid named Sarah. Uncle Dalmahoy, who happened just then to be staying in the house, had his manservant, who acted as groom to him, but who at that time was assisting to wait at table, etc. He was an honest, trustworthy man, though occasionally he yielded to the besetting sin of his class, and became for the time incapable of attending to anything. There was a nurse, a respectable elderly woman, whose time was fully occupied with my aunt, Mrs Moore Campbell, and her infant; there was also another woman servant, a laundress, but I forget if there was a man or woman cook. The kitchen, laundry, and servants' rooms were quite detached from the house and from each other, forming altogether three sides of a square; further back was a large stable built of slabs and covered with bark. Those were very primitive times.

The house was built on the slope of a hill and was of brick. It consisted of four good-sized rooms divided by a wide passage, and two veranda rooms. In front and on half of each side there was a deep veranda raised five or six steps from the ground, the back door being level with the ground; the veranda rooms opened off the veranda and were the same width. In some houses these rooms had a door leading into the back rooms of the house, but this was not the case at the White Rock.

On the evening in question we were all assembled in the only public room (it being too cold for us to sit in the veranda, which in that climate often supplies the place of a second room). I was sent a message to my mother's room, which lay immediately behind, and I there found Sarah, the housemaid, kneeling before an open trunk. I did not speak to her, but asked on my return if she had been sent to look for anything. My mother went to see what she was doing, and came back at once saying there was no one in the room, but she missed from it a large camphorwood trunk in which she kept her best dresses, jewels, and other valuables.

The gentlemen went to assure themselves that the box was not there. The servants were called in—all were at hand, and apparently quite ignorant of any theft. Sarah in particular was very much concerned about it, and denied that she had opened the other trunk, though she owned to having been in the bed-room a few minutes before, when she was sure that all was right. As the loss was a serious one, Adams, Uncle Dalmahoy's groom, was at once despatched to Bathurst for the mounted police, the distance, I think, being about four miles.

In a very short time Captain C—— and two troopers arrived. They examined the houses and cross-questioned the servants, but without gaining the slightest information. They then visited a cottage about a quarter of a mile distant, at the foot of the slope on which the house was built, and quite near the river. There they found three or four people sitting quietly, who expressed much astonishment and interest at hearing of the robbery. As it was quite dark nothing more could be done that night.

Next morning the troopers came out again, and Sarah now gave a rather garbled tale of having seen two strangers the evening before who had passed the house and gone towards the river and disappeared, going up the river and not towards the cottage before-mentioned. The ground was hard and stony round the house, and unenclosed, so there was no way of tracing any footsteps. There was no doubt that the trunk had been taken out by the back door, the supposition being that someone in or belonging to the house had there handed it over to his or her accomplices, as when the robbery was first discovered no one was missing.

For two days search was made in every likely and unlikely spot, and a strict watch kept upon the cottage, about whose inhabitants the police did not seem to be quite satisfied, but they showed no excitement and went about their usual occupations, apparently unconscious that they were suspected. On the third morning when we were at breakfast, an old man, who lived at the opposite side of the river and farmed his own ground, came up to the front door and asked to see one of the ladies, so my mother went to speak to him, and to her surprise, he produced a China crepe shawl belonging to her, which had been in the missing trunk. He said that early in the morning he had noticed some crows collecting in one of his fields, and thought from the way they were going on that there must be some dead animal there, but on going to the spot he found only this shawl, which he supposed had attracted them by its pink colour; and hearing that a lady at the White Rock had been robbed, he came to inquire if that article belonged to her.

Here was a clue; it was evident that the box had been opened in the neighbourhood, and most likely at our side of the river, as there was neither tree or shelter on the other side, near where the shawl had been found. We followed farmer Hall to the spot, then returned and searched on the bank and bed of the river, which in some places was nearly dry, though there were many deep pools and stretches of deep water. In one part there was a sort of island where the stream divided, and must have flowed for years in separate channels, for there were several good-sized trees of casuarina or swamp-oak growing among the driftwood and stones. It was quite a narrow strip with no vegetation. Here, strange to say, the trunk was found, come upon quite unexpectedly by one of the party.

It was not hidden, but just set down by a tree, and concealed by the stones and roots, which were much of the same size and colour. The box had been broken open but was closed, and much that it had contained was still left in it, noticeably two unmade-up pieces of silk, and one very handsome silk dress. The jewel box and all it contained had been taken, also a gold watch and chain. The trunk was carried home in triumph and the police were again called in, but they could learn nothing further

of the robbers.

It was two or three months before we heard anything more of the matter, but eventually all was explained, and most of the things recovered, and with them some other things that had also been stolen, one being a ring that a lady friend staying at the White Rock had missed and supposed she had dropped off her finger. This is how the discovery came about. A woman travelling to Sydney by the coach asked someone to wind her watch as she had lost the key. The watch was a handsome gold one, with a long chain attached, as was then the fashion. When a key was handed to her she did not know how to use it.

As the same woman took a brooch to be mended which answered the description of one of those stolen, the police were put on her track and found she had all the missing jewellery still in her possession. It had been baked at once into a damper, a kind of large unleavened loaf commonly used in the bush, and so hidden had more than once passed under the eyes of the police, for the trunk had been taken to the cottage first suspected and searched. Sarah and a friend had carried the trunk out of the bedroom and given it to two men who were waiting for it outside. My having discovered her had nearly caused the failure of the whole plan, as they had scarcely left the house when the trunk was missed. They hastened down the hill and opened it the moment they reached the cottage, and at once baked the jewels into the damper.

Two men who were accomplices and who had warned them that the loss of the box had been discovered, carried it at once to the bed of the river, and set it down where it was afterwards found. The others had hardly settled down in the cottage when the police paid them their first visit, and as they had not dared to go again to the river, they failed to secure the rest of their booty. The accomplices who carried off the trunk had helped themselves to some things, but in their hurry had dropped the pink crepe shawl after they had crossed the river in their homeward flight. Sarah and three others were tried and punished for the robbery, which had been instigated and planned by her.

Chapter

2

JOURNEY BY
BULLOCK DRAY

I SHALL NOW MAKE some extracts from an old journal which I
began to keep about January 1839. I was then more than
twelve years old, my sister nine and a half, and two happy,
contented children we were with every reason to be so.

At that time we were alone at home with mamma and our
governess, dear papa, who continued very delicate, having gone
again to Sydney to consult a doctor there. We were expecting
him back, when a letter came to say that he was not so well, and
had been advised to spend the winter at Port Macquarie. His
brother, Major Innes, had kindly asked us all to stay at Lake
Innes, and arrangements were being made for us to start as
soon as possible. This was indeed important news, for though
such a journey had sometimes been spoken of it was not
expected that it would ever take place, but now our dear father
was ill, and we thought this visit to the seaside would be
sure to make him well again, so all was bustle and pleasant
preparation. Margaret and I in our own way were very busy
too, our gardens and various pets taking up every spare moment
from needlework and lessons.

How well I remember one lovely moonlight night sometime
in February—the moon was at its full, the air soft and balmy,

fragrant with the scent of many flowers—Margaret and I had gone to bed leaving our window which opened on to the veranda quite open, when we heard the sound of wheels and presently a gig drove past and stopped. We were instantly in the veranda and clinging round the dear traveller's neck, for a moment not observing that he had a companion with him. Soon we were arrayed in more suitable costumes and seated in the dining-room. We sat up very late, and papa gave us each a handsomely bound Annual which he had brought from Sydney for us, and with which we were much delighted.

I shall now give you the best account I can of our journey which was delayed till the beginning of March.

The day before we started a dray was sent off with a tent and provisions of all sorts for us as we expected to spend two nights in the bush before arriving at the place about twenty miles distant where a carriage and horses were awaiting our arrival to convey us more comfortably and rapidly on our journey to Sydney. It was a lovely morning in the first week in March when we set off in a large and comfortable carriage and five, in other words a large dray well piled with mattresses and pillows, and drawn by five strong bullocks. A steady old driver walked at one side, carrying a long-handled whip which he waved over them, or cracked cheerfully from time to time, another man following ready to assist in any way. Miss Smith, Margaret and I were seated in state in the dray, papa and mamma followed in the gig, a friend and our groom rode.

Ours certainly was a very slow conveyance, but we had only nine miles to go, and really a dray is not a rough carriage, for the great wheels move so slowly and seem so little affected by going over a stone, or sinking into a wide rut, that we never thought of being afraid. The gig soon flew past us, and on our arrival at Coco Creek, where we were to encamp for the night, we found the tent pitched in a wild but sheltered spot, near some tall swamp-oak trees, the branches of which were waving mournfully in a gentle breeze.

Two bright fires were soon kindled. The horses were tethered to the neighbouring trees, or were set loose with hobbles on, which rattled as they made their way to the water-holes in the bed of the creek, forsaking for a time the provender that had been brought for them, the bullocks also moving leisurely in the same direction. A carpet was soon spread under the tent and two trunks set as tables near the entrance. On them we spread a snowy cloth and began with eager haste to arrange the good things that had been so liberally provided for our refreshment. It was not like the bush scenes I have enjoyed both before and since, for we had taken everything we could think of to make us comfortable.

The little brass kettle was soon handed up with tea, a basin of sugar and a bottle of milk, while wine was drawn for those who preferred it. The first evening all our provisions were cold, but a coop with some plump chickens in it promised that if we should be detained longer than we expected we need not starve. The weather was still too hot for us to carry with us any uncooked supplies.

As soon as our repast was ended we had to get our beds ready, and many were the discussions as to where our heads should be and where they should not be. All being satisfactorily arranged, we retired to rest, and in a few minutes I forgot that I was not in my own snug bed, and slept profoundly till roused by the men lighting the fires and bringing in the cattle. We soon started up, and, seizing clothes and towels, flew to bathe in the clear, cool stream. We soon found a sheltered palm, and there arrayed ourselves as expeditiously as possible.

How well I remember kneeling on the soft green bank to say my morning prayer. There are times when even the most thoughtless must feel impressed by the omnipotence and omnipresence of God. I shall never forget that morning prayer under the shade of the green swamp-oak trees in the wild bush. Returning to our tent, we made a hearty breakfast. Everything was soon packed, the horses harnessed, the patient bullocks yoked together, and it was still early when we resumed our journey, leaving few traces of our last night's resting place but the smouldering fires and the trodden-down grass. This was all very delightful: as yet we had had no difficulties.

Before I proceed I must explain that there were only two ways of leaving our happy valley (unless by a very circuitous route) as it was entirely surrounded by mountains.

One of these roads was known as "The Hole", the other as "The Peak". "The Hole" was the best as well as the shortest way, but only available for persons walking or on horseback, for there was one tremendous hill up and down which no vehicle could be taken, and down which no one could ride. We were consequently obliged to travel by "The Peak", which was for many miles a succession of hills and hollows and dangerous sidelines. We were not long in arriving at a steep hill designated "The First Pinch". Here we all dismounted and scrambled up as best we could, while the dray followed, the men cracking their whips and shouting to the bullocks.

At every pause they made, and these were not infrequent, someone was ready with a large stone to stop the wheel from slipping backward. The gig was light, and two horses drew it up with comparative ease, but the poor bullocks laboured up with the heavy dray. Meanwhile we walked on, loading ourselves with flowers and berries, a branch of some bright evergreen that had attracted our attention, or perhaps a handful of the flinty and variegated stones over which we were walking, all to be thrown away at the next steep hill, where hands and feet were in requisition. Sometimes one of us would be entrusted with a horse to hold or lead, not at all an easy task.

Here and there was a deep gully between the steep hills, and perhaps a few hundred yards of level ground would delight us after our labours. In one of these places we rested for a short time, but were obliged to press on owing to the great want of water, as none was to be found where we halted. Fortunately we had brought with us a keg and a large stone jar full of water, and as we had also some light wine and some home-made beer, we felt no anxiety about ourselves, and we still hoped that the cattle would be able to find some water-hole at which to refresh themselves. Mamma and Miss Smith rambled on, while we children rested and had a little drive in the gig to overtake them; it felt like flying after our late creeping pace, but we did not long enjoy this flight, as more hills presented themselves, and we again scrambled up to watch the progress of the rest of the party.

I have hitherto spoken of the difficulty of going up a hill, but going down, especially for a loaded dray, was quite as difficult; the wheel had to be locked, that is prevented from turning, by a chain which fastened it to the dray, which is then dragged the hill with a grating sound and a tremulous motion of the dray and its contents. If the descent happened to be long, a small tree was often cut down and fastened behind the dray, thus adding to its weight and so keeping it back. It was astonishing the number of these trees to be seen lying at the foot of some of these steep hills which had been brought down in this way and were of no further use.

But to return to ourselves, the sun was fast declining and we began to fear that we should not be able to reach Ely or Erly Flat, the place we had intended to stop at, and where we were sure of a good supply of water, yet everyone was anxious to get on, as the want of water, even for one night, is a most serious evil, and especially so after a day of fatigue such as ours had been. The point was, however, settled for us by some part of the dray or harness giving way. I forget now the immediate cause, but I know that the effect was that our stone jar was broken, and all the precious water it contained of course was lost, and that we were compelled to stay where we were till the next day.

Deep were the lamentations over the broken jar. Unless one has experienced something similar one can scarcely realize our dismay at the loss of our only sure supply of water. As it was impossible to reach the Flat, our only hope lay in the Reedy Gully, an old camping place about half a mile off. We managed to arrive there before dark, and while some attended to the animals and lit the fires, others set off in quest of water. We were all very thirsty, wine we could not drink, and the beer had been given to the men, who were worse off than we, from being unable to indulge in their usual and most refreshing quart-pots full of tea. We waited for some time hoping for water.

At length the first party returned, their little keg still empty. Then we ate our supper, but would have given it all for a little water. Suddenly we remembered that there was a box of grapes we were taking to a friend on the way. The grapes had been bagged on the vines and so kept fresh after all the others were finished. At first we were delighted with them, but they were so very ripe and sweet we were soon more thirsty than ever. At last, tired and dispirited we went to bed and happily were soon sound asleep.

About midnight we were awakened with the joyful cry of "Water, water!". A second party had gone out and now returned in triumph with their keg full. They kindly brought some to us first, and we thankfully took a few mouthfuls. Next morning we rose with the pleasant hope of getting some tea. Great was our surprise on looking into the pannikin in which the water had been brought to us to see nothing but green slime, and that with a very offensive smell. We could not bear to think that we had tasted it, for now all declared we would rather go with faces and hands unwashed than touch such stuff.

However, a night's rest had very much refreshed us, and as we had got over the most difficult part of the road we set out again in high spirits. The poor horses and bullocks looked anything but cheerful, though refreshed to a certain extent by a heavy dew. It really was wonderful to see them some hours after when we came near some water-holes, how they quickened their paces and seemed impatient to reach them. We wondered if, as most of them had travelled on the road before, they had sufficient instinct to remember it as a place always well supplied with good water.

Here we rested for a few hours and that night reached the place where the carriage was waiting for us. It was then known

as the "Water Holes", there being a succession of ponds or small lagoons prettily situated at the roadside. I remember seeing some lovely waterlilies floating on these ponds. There was a good hut there, a sort of accommodation house, some paddock and a nice little garden, but as we had every convenience for camping out, and the weather was good, we did not go to the house, but we got some fresh supplies and new milk from the owner.

This, though not a public house, was a place of entertainment, and there were a great many drays encamped near the ponds, some taking down bales of wool, others taking back supplies from Sydney to distant stations. The place was a sort of junction where roads met from various distant up-country stations. It really was astonishing to see some of the large wool drays how they were packed, and often on the top of all was to be seen a woman and two or three small children. How they got up was a mystery to me, and being up, how they travelled on such roads and met with so few accidents was still more

"The place was a sort
of junction where roads meet."

wonderful. Each dray was drawn by from eight to twelve
bullocks, in charge of a driver and another man.

We had now emerged into comparatively civilized regions,
and next morning had everything that was to be sent home
again packed into one of the drays, which at once started back
by the road we had so lately come. The other dray went on
to Sydney with our luggage, etc., we taking with us in the
carriage only what was absolutely necessary for the journey.
We soon set off at a smart pace, my father following in the gig
with the groom. We stopped for luncheon at Cullen Bullen,
where we were most kindly received by Dr Dalhunty, his
mother and sister. It was a very pretty place, and quite my ideal
of a country home. I am told that now it has gone to ruin,
the owner dead, the family scattered, and the place sold.

We were so late in resuming our journey that the sun had
set before we reached the inn at which we were to stop that
night. This was a large, bare-looking house at the junction of
our road with that from Bathurst, long known and celebrated

JOURNEY BY BULLOCK DRAY

as Malachi Ryan's, but its celebrity was not flattering, as, though not haunted by ghosts, it was so infested with creatures more likely to disturb one's rest that I wonder now why anyone stopped a night there. One traveller declared he had been dragged out of bed, another kept up a continual fight to prevent himself from being devoured alive, and a nervous lady, being left alone with her invisible tormentors, could think of no expedient save that of ringing a small hand-bell all the weary night to frighten them off.

To add to our discomfort on arriving at this wretched place, the gig had not overtaken us, though we had waited several times in the hope of it coming up, and mamma was getting very anxious, though we could not say what was to be apprehended. As time wore on our anxiety became painful when (it cannot be said to relieve our fears) dear papa walked in, but so pale and lame, that we saw at once he had met with an accident. He had indeed had a most wonderful escape. A road gang was at that time making in one part of the road a new piece some feet lower than the old, and had neglected to put a paling along the side of the upper road. Over this bank the horse had stepped in the uncertain moonlight, drawing the gig down after him. It was a miracle that they were not all killed.

Poor papa was very much bruised and shaken, which in his weak state of health was very alarming. The man with him was not very much hurt, but the horse, a splendid creature, we feared could not recover. However, with great care and attention, he became in time as well as ever. The gig was smashed to pieces. Fortunately the place where the accident happened was quite near the inn. We spent there a miserable night, but were able to leave next morning. Miss Smith had to sit on the box of the carriage to leave more room inside, and in this way we reached Penrith on the third or fourth day. We there crossed the Nepean river in a punt, and stopped the night in a large and comfortable inn. Of the scenery on the road I cannot remember anything, as we were shut up in a close carriage, and could only hope at some future time to see it under more favourable circumstances.

Our last day's journey was from Penrith to Liverpool, rather off the direct route to Sydney, which lay through Parramatta by the western road. We children and Miss Smith were to be left at Mary Vale, near Liverpool, with my aunt Mrs Macleod, while our parents went on to Sydney to await the arrival of our dray with our luggage, and to complete the arrangements necessary for our voyage and stay at Port Macquarie. It was St Patrick's day, and several carriages passed us taking people to Sydney to attend a grand ball given on the occasion by the sons of Erin. I remember wondering if I would ever go to a ball, and thinking it such a very grand event.

Arrived at Mary Vale, we found that my aunt and her two eldest daughters had gone to the ball, from which they returned next day. We spent two or three weeks with them very pleasantly. There was a large family of all ages, and my aunt was most kind and indulgent to us all. We went often to Liverpool, where we were always most kindly welcomed by Mrs Andrew Allan (*née* Bayley), a very beautiful woman, who looked most interesting in her widow's cap, surrounded by her six beautiful children, and it was a great joy to us to take tea with them. We visited, also, a Colonel and Mrs Mackenzie; one of their girls was about my own age, and we struck up a warm but short-lived friendship.

We remained at Mary Vale till the steamer was advertised to sail for Port Macquarie, when we proceeded to Sydney, but were there detained for several days by stormy weather. We stopped at the old Royal Hotel,[1] George Street, and part of the time had rooms opposite, which were quieter. We had some shopping to do for ourselves, which was a great treat, and mamma got us pretty grey silk pelisses, and neat poke bonnets of fine straw, trimmed with straw-coloured ribbon.

---

[1] The hotel had just been altered by John Verge. It was burnt down in 1840, but was later rebuilt.

Chapter

3

BY SEA
TO PORT MACQUARIE

IT WAS THE MIDDLE of April before the important day arrived on which for the first time we went to sea. We had not made up our minds that we would be very ill, and partly in consequence felt very well, and slept till we reached Newcastle; we went on board very late, and no doubt were asleep before we left Sydney harbour.

At Newcastle the steamer stopped to take in coal for that and the return voyage, so after a good breakfast we landed and walked up to the little white church[1] on the hill. From the ground on the north side there was a splendid view, looking straight across the harbour to the north shore, up the river, and to Nobby's on the right. Nobby's was a little island at the entrance to the harbour on which there was a lighthouse, and to it the Government meant to make a breakwater, in the hope of improving the harbour by contracting and deepening the entrance. We saw a chain gang at work, but somehow this compulsory labour never seemed to effect much. We put out from Newcastle about twelve o'clock and spent a wretched day at sea.

Next morning we arrived off Port Macquarie, crossed the bar without difficulty, and on landing found my uncle's carriage

[1] It was on the site of the present Cathedral.

waiting to convey us to Lake Innes, a distance of some seven miles. My dear, kind uncle Major Innes was himself driving. My aunt received us most kindly, and we were charmed with the beauty of the place and our surroundings. The family then consisted of my uncle and aunt, their two little girls, a boy about a year old, and our aunt Barbara Innes, who had come from Scotland some time before for the benefit of her health. She was tall and very handsome, and afterwards married in April 1842 Mr George Macleay, a brother of my aunt, Mrs Innes.

We spent at this time seven months at Lake Innes. At first our dear invalid benefitted so much by the change of air and scene, that as he walked about the lovely gardens, or drove quietly to the beach with my mother and aunt, we flattered ourselves that he would be soon quite restored to health. We girls soon settled into our usual routine of daily lessons, sitting either in the day-nursery or deep veranda on to which it opened.

My cousins spent most of their time out of doors. Gustavus had a Scotch nurse, who I remember used to work at what she called "Ayrshire flowering". She used two little wooden hoops, over one she stretched the muslin on which she was going to work, and the outer hoop was then slipped over the muslin and kept all firm. The girls had a governess, Miss Paine by name, a truly good woman, but more than eccentric. She was devoted to my cousin Gordina, then a dear little girl of four, and I have no doubt her teaching influenced the child's whole life, for she was different from other people from her earliest years, and as near perfection as mortals can attain. Dido, on the other hand, was somewhat under the influence of a lady who came every week to give music lessons, and stayed always one night.

This lady had been known to Aunt Barbara under very different circumstances. She was the daughter of a Baronet and made a very unfortunate marriage, her husband being finally "sent" to the Colony, and was then a "Special" at Port Macquarie. Being a man of good education he was employed there as a clerk. She had dutifully followed him, and they lived together in a pretty little cottage near the settlement. I never saw him, nor do I know his proper name. People situated as they were naturally adopted an alias. She was a bright little woman, and the weekly visit to the Lake made a pleasant break in her dull and changed life.

We all went very often to the beach, which was distant almost two miles from the house. I shall never forget the first time I went there, and my first view of the great Pacific Ocean, and the rolling surf, as it boiled and foamed and then spread peacefully over the sparkling yellow sands. I was very ill soon after we went to the Lake, and was confined to bed for some days. I then first became acquainted with our dear old friend Dr Stacey. When I was able to go out again our first drive was to the beach. I was not allowed to go down to the sand, but rested on shawls and cushions under a sheltering tree. There I first beheld the open ocean, looking due east over the wide Pacific. I had lately been on the sea, but as we went below while still in the harbour, and remained there till we were ready to land, I had not realized its vastness.

Early in August my father was so well that he proposed that we should all return home the following month in the early spring. My uncle went up to Sydney to arrange about a steamer calling for us; but alas, our hopes were doomed to speedy disappointment. Our dear invalid became suddenly worse, and, after suffering much for a few days, died on the 17th August, aged thirty-seven, and while my uncle was still absent. This was indeed a terrible blow to us, and changed all our plans. In November it was settled that we should return for a time to our home, Miss Smith to remain in Sydney and follow us later on. This, I may here say, she did not do, but married soon after, and we at Capita ran wild for nearly eighteen months. Then we went to live at Parramatta, where for nearly two years we attended a day school, and finally in January 1841 returned to Lake Innes.

I quite well remember our return voyage to Sydney in November 1839. It was in a tiny sailing vessel called the *Elizabeth*

Cohen, crowded with passengers, and sick and miserable we all were. Two people played cribbage loud and long in the cabin off which our little den opened. I had never heard of the game, and wondered much what they could be talking about. The steward was a very superior man and very attentive to us; he was, in fact, part owner of the schooner, and when we arrived in Sydney late on Sunday evening, and no one came to meet us, he insisted on our going to his house for the night, and his nice, pretty little wife made us very comfortable.

Early next morning Uncle Dalmahoy Campbell came for us. He had already been to the schooner in search of us, and had there secured our luggage. He took us to the Royal Hotel, where some other friends were staying, and we remained for two or three days. While we were there Aunt M'Leod's baby boy was christened by Dr M'Garvie "Charles Colin". It was a sad christening; his mother had died only a few weeks before, and Aunt Isabella, who was with her at the time, had promised to take the baby and his sister Williamina, aged about eight, home with her to the Wallombi[1] for a time. Mamma offered to take her name daughter, Lorn Edith, with us to Capita, a temporary break up of the M'Leod family being necessary, as Mary Vale was let to other tenants, and all their plans were changed. Before they moved we spent a week or two with them again.

My two grown-up cousins were very kind to us, but it was a sad and changed household since our last visit, and we were only too well able to sympathize with them. I was then a very over-grown girl of thirteen, five feet eight and a half inches in height, and not very strong; Margaret was ten, and stout, fair, and rosy. Uncle Dalmahoy came with us to Mary Vale to see his nieces, and to make arrangements for our journey back to Capita. He had not long returned from an overland journey to Adelaide, one of the first ever made with cattle, and one which I fancy was very successful. Either then or on a second journey Mr Evelyn Sturt, a brother of the explorer, was his companion.

[1] Now spelt Wollombi. Annabella also spells it Woollombi.

42

We started from Liverpool about the end of November in a neat caravan, a sort of spring cart, with a high arched frame above, covered with canvas, Uncle Dalmahoy driving in it his beautiful grey horse Block, mamma sitting beside him, and we two girls and our little cousin inside. We went by the usual route known as the Western Road, stopping first at Penrith, then up Lapstone hill to Victoria and Hartley. Near the latter place we left the main road to Bathurst by Mount Lambie, and turned into the Mudgee road, thus avoiding Malachi Ryan's comfortless inn.

That night we arrived at Wallerowang, the residence of our good friends Mr and Mrs James Walker. I do not remember having been there before, as they were absent when we went to Sydney, but my parents had often stopped there when Mr Walker was a bachelor. Some years before this he went home and had quite lately returned, bringing with him from Scotland a very charming wife and two little girls. She was most kind and hospitable to us, and in the evening sang some beautiful old Scotch songs, among them "The Flowers of the Forest", which I heard then for the first time. The eldest girl, Allison, was big enough to ride on a pretty little donkey, so next day several donkeys were brought up for our amusement, and we scampered about on them with much satisfaction to ourselves. Mr David Archer, who was staying at Wallerowang, was most kind and patient in mounting us and helping to manage our steeds. He was going to Louie, a cattle station of Mr Walker's on the Castlereagh River, and, fortunately for us, it was arranged that he should go with us by Capita, and so help us on our journey round the Peak.

We rested at Wallerowang for some days, and our groom came to us from Glen Alice, bringing with him a good strong horse, so Uncle Dalmahoy determined to make an effort to make the whole journey in one long day; the distance was not really great, not more than thirty-five miles, but the difficulty lay in the bad road. The days were long and the moon at its full, so we set off very early, driving our two good horses out-rigger

BY SEA TO PORT MACQUARIE

fashion, not at all a good plan, I think, especially on such bad roads.

However, all went well till we had gone nearly half way, when we had to descend a very steep hill. There were so many worse yet to come, where we would be obliged to walk, that my uncle persuaded us to remain in the caravan, unfortunately as it turned out, for an important piece of the harness broke and the horses became restive and plunged. Mamma was thrown out on to the back of one of them, but escaped quite unhurt, and my uncle held them steady by main strength till Mr Archer helped us out at the back of the van. After that the horses made a bolt. One of the shafts was broken, and a wheel so injured that it was impossible for us to go any further with it. Most provi dentially we had just passed a neat little spring cart and horse, driven by an old man named Jack Hall, who was well known on the road as a sort of hawker and carrier of light goods. His cart was nearly empty, so he agreed to take us on to Capita, and we transferred at once to his care our not very bulky luggage, and started again at a slow pace, leaving the gentlemen to take the caravan to a place of safety at a roadside hut in the neighbourhood.

What a weary journey that was. Our friend Jack Hall preferred keeping his own steady old horse in the shafts to making use of one of our fiery steeds, so he was helped up the hills, and the cart held back going down till at last we reached in safety the foot of the much dreaded "First Pinch", after which the road was fairly good. We had one other misadventure before this point was reached. At a steep side line ending in a sharp turn and a deep gully, in spite of every effort the cart upset. Of course, there was no one in it, and no great harm was done, but we got a great fright. Our two horses were given to me to hold, while all hands helped to right the cart, and set free the fallen horse, which lay helplessly on its back, so complete was the overturn.

The horses I held became restive, plunged and neighed, and finally pulled their bridles out of my hands. I was terrified, fearing they would be lost, even if they did not hurt themselves or us, but they were soon caught, and then I was mounted on Mr Archer's huge but quiet animal. There was a valise strapped in front of the saddle, and the off side stirrup was thrown over to support my right foot, the left foot resting firmly in the near side stirrup leather. It was a long and weary ride, eerie too in the pale moonlight, which threw strange shadows across our path. Mamma sat with the children in the cart, tired too, but always patient.

At last, about midnight, we found ourselves in safety at our own door. Mr and Mrs Duncan, our overseer and his wife, and our Highland maidservant, who were living in the house in our absence, had gone to bed, having given up all expectations of seeing us that night, but they soon roused up and gave us a warm welcome and a good supper, which was much required, after which, worn and weary, we soon retired to rest.

Next morning Uncle Dalmahoy was very tired and much bruised and strained from his great exertions in holding back the horses at the time the harness broke; we felt we owed our lives to his great strength and bravery. My mother busied herself in attending on him, which helped to turn her thoughts from our sad home-coming. He remained with us for a week or two, and helped my mother in making such arrangements as were necessary: he and my uncle, Major Innes, were our guardians, named by my father. I have heard that his will was never read, as the office in Sydney in which it was left was burned down, and most of the papers kept in it destroyed.

We soon settled down in our solitary home, cheered by the pleasant prospect of a visit from my aunt, Mrs Arthur Ranken, who had promised to come with her children from their home at Glen Logan, Lachlan River, and stay with us while my uncle was absent on a journey to Port Philip (now Victoria). They came early in 1840, and remained with us most of the time till we left Glen Alice for good in April 1841, the children being a great joy to me, especially George, the eldest boy.

I have an old journal detailing all the interests and occupations of these months, but will not enlarge upon them here, although my recollections are very pleasant of the primitive way in which we lived. Still I cannot altogether omit a short sketch of our doings. We were still very remote from any settlement, and there was no station of any importance near us; but we now had half-yearly visits from the Rev. Colin Stewart, a most worthy and devoted Presbyterian minister. He lived near Hartley, but spent most of his time in travelling through the country. When he came to us we had a service in the veranda, attended by all who could possibly come. On one occasion Mrs Maclean came from Warrangee to have her baby christened. The service was in Gaelic, and the child was called Ian, but instead of keeping to that pretty Highland name he was afterwards called Jonathan, his father and an uncle being named John. Occasionally we went over to Warrangee to see the family. They had come out from Skye to claim the property on the death of their relative, Mr John Maclean, who was drowned at Norfolk Island, and were now comfortably settled there. Mrs Maclean often came over to consult my mother, who spoke Gaelic perfectly, and they had very little English.

We were very much thrown on our own resources. My sister and I had some lessons to do most days, and we drew and practised by fits and starts, albeit much at our own sweet will. I read greedily such books as we possessed, chiefly the *Waverley Novels,* which then and always interested me. I read most of them aloud as well as to myself. We had Cooper's novels also, which fascinated me then, but somehow I have never read them since, and have no wish to do so. I feel I would not now be in sympathy with them. I regret that some of the books we had were denied to us, among them Shakespeare, which seems strange to me now, but my mother was old-fashioned in her ideas and somewhat of a disciplinarian. We spent much of our time out of doors, where our interests were very varied, in the fields and gardens, and among all living creatures, from the native blacks, who often came about the place, to the birds and insects we met with in our walks.

We grew our own wheat, and the sowing, reaping, and grinding in steel handmills interested us, and I may say that we watched the rise and progress of our bread from the time our seed was sown till it came out of the oven. The making of potato flour was another great joy. We watched also the manufacture of our candles, dips and moulds, from the melting and hardening of the fat to the lighting of the wicks, and were proud to assist in such a share of the work as was permitted to us.

The dairy was another great interest, and we often rose early to go with our little cousins to the milking yard for mugs of new milk, warm and frothy, from our favourite cows. Butter and cheese were made for home use, and occasionally for the Sydney market. We had a variety of jams and jellies, dried apples and peaches, and preserved grapes for use till late in the season by covering them with paper bags while still on the vines, which bags we had, of course, to make. We had a great variety of poultry, and more eggs that we could possibly use. Delicious cakes were of every day use, sugar being the only thing we had to buy.

Our Highland maid was a famous baker of bread, and made also delightful rolls and scones. Sometimes we children made a cake and had it baked in primitive fashion on the hot hearth under an inverted pot with hot coals placed on the top. Sometimes we had a damper, which is always best when made from steel-mill flour, and must be baked on the hot hearth and covered with wood ashes. It is a kind of unleavened bread made like a large round scone two or three inches thick.

Our house was very well furnished, and we had had great pleasure in seeing the manufacture of much of the furniture from a large log of cedar which was brought up from Sydney in one of our own drays while the house was being built. There was a saw pit not far from the house, and on to the frame which surrounded it the log of cedar was rolled, and there cut into boards of the required thickness. These boards were seasoned for the proper time, and then worked up by a cabinetmaker, who was engaged from Sydney to make what was required.

He was assisted by our carpenter, George Miller. They had good designs to work from, and the result was a handsome sideboard, a large wardrobe, a chest of drawers, and other things. My mother had a very pretty davenport which was bought in Sydney at the sale of things belonging to a Mr Kenworthy, an American, from whom my father bought also a number of delightful books.

In writing of these old days, I may here add that in after years people have often asked me about our bush life, and what they were pleased to call "those terrible times", when there were only convict servants. I do not remember them as terrible times at all. We were always well and kindly served, and I can even now recall to mind the names and appearance of some of those who, if they left their country for their country's good, were often sent out for very small offences, and found comfort and prosperity in the distant land to which they had been banished. No doubt there were some sad exceptions, but these people would not have done well anywhere. I was eight years old when I came home from school to Glen Alice, and for six years after that we lived there with only convict servants, excepting that during the last two years we had our Highland maid, whom I have before mentioned, and who might have been called lady's

"We soon settled down in our solitary home."

maid had such a luxury been known in our benighted wilds.

Our chief favourite was our old gardener, a perfectly honest, kindly man. He worked early and late, and was always ready to help up with our gardens. He delighted in bringing in the first ripe fruit, and never failed to present us with a Sunday posy. He was an Englishman, and elderly even when I first remember him. I have since been told that his offence was bigamy, then punished by transportation for life. When he left Glen Alice he went to Wallerowang and there helped to form a very pretty garden, which I saw many years afterwards, but the busy hands that had planted it were at rest, our old gardener having died in the service of our friends, Mr and Mrs James Walker. In the same hut with the gardener lived the shoemaker, also an Englishman, very civil and obliging, but only seen by us when sent for, as he worked for others besides our people, and remained on after he got his "ticket-of-leave". We had a blacksmith, an excellent workman, quiet and respectable, and we often looked in to see him at work at his forge, which was in a large commodious shed, in which were fixed two steel hand-mills for grinding wheat. When the blacksmith got his freedom he married our laundress, a goodlooking, clever woman, and they went to a distant part of the country, where no doubt their descendants are doing well.

George, the groom, also English, was an especial favourite. He always treated me as if I were a little princess, and took the greatest pains about breaking in a horse for me. The merits of the said horse were so great that a large price was offered for him, and he was sold, and I had again to content myself with our old pony. I don't know what became of George; there was another of the same name from Aberdeen, before this time, a poet and a ne'er-do-weel. I mentioned him before. We had also George Miller, a Scotchman, a carpenter, and a very decent man, who helped to build our house. He made us a beautiful bedstead for our dolls, and many other charming, if clumsy toys, which delighted us. At one time our cook was an old soldier, clean and orderly. He came to grief for striking his superior officer, a corporal, who probably was not more sober at the time than himself. When with us he had no opportunity of indulging in anything stronger than tea, and I never heard of Macguire as otherwise than well behaved. He was the only Irishman with us at that time, but later on many were sent to the country for rioting, and what may be called political offences.

We had two bullock drivers who also did the farm work. When the drays went to Sydney, which they did every spring immediately after shearing so as to be back by Christmas, two other men accompanied them for protection, and to help with the bullocks, camp fires, etc. It was considered a great favour to be allowed to go. Once the gardener went and brought back a number of trees and vine cuttings from the botanical and other gardens. My mother was a devoted gardener, and every year we had many beautiful annuals in flower, and many an hour we devoted to watering them and sheltering them from the hot sun. We had also two or three shepherds and their hut keepers, who came to the home station for rations, clothing, etc.: sometimes the stores were sent out to them. Dan Taylor was the old shepherd's name. He brought us in more than one little lamb to be fed and petted, and then to our grief taken back to the flock, where they soon forgot us.

There was one unsatisfactory individual among our men, Hutchison by name. He ran away, or took the bush, which was the expression commonly used for such escapades. He did not become a bushranger, as he was soon caught and sent back to the prisoners' barracks, and we saw him no more. Before that we had two Englishmen, father and son, poachers, very handsome men, but surly. They were not long with us. I do not remember any others that were not quite satisfactory.

I must not omit to mention James Horn, a very little man, but with a large heart and a brave spirit. On one occasion, the Christmas after my father's death, when we were having but a sad time at Glen Alice, a large supply of spirits had arrived with other stores at a neighbouring station where there was only an overseer in charge. It was the custom to give a dinner and some spirits to the men on Christmas day. Somehow they had got too much spirits, and the consequence was they broke into the store and took more. A scene of riot and confusion followed, in which some Irishmen vowed that they would take the lives of the Englishmen present. Our shoemaker, who was among the number, made his escape, and, as soon as he could, made for his own hut, which was perhaps two miles distant through the bush. Horn was at that time living with him and the old gardener, and at once undertook to come up to the house (about half a mile further) to warn us of possible danger, and to protect us in case the mad creatures should make their way over to us; they knew that we had wine in the cellar, and that we were a helpless household. My aunt, Mrs Ranken, was with us, and two young children, a little Highland nurse, and a prisoner woman. Our own party was my mother, my sister, and myself, our cousin Edith M'Leod, Christina, our Highland maid, and a prisoner woman—in all, five women, four girls, and two little children. I shall never forget our fear and anxiety when Horn came up and told his tale. It was a bright moonlight night, excessively hot, even the veranda felt airless, being sheltered by creepers, so we had made ourselves seats out-of-doors with some cedar planks that had been set up against the end of the house to season for future use. There we were seated about nine o'clock when Horn arrived breathless, to say that the shoemaker had escaped from Umbiella with his life and was much hurt, and that the men from there were in pursuit of him.

He told how the gardener and he were barricading themselves in their hut, and he had come up to warn and protect us. We could do nothing, so we sat a while longer in the moonlight, starting at every sound, and then we girls were sent to bed, the elders sitting up till daylight. Horn walked round the house from time to time all night, but no one came near to alarm or disturb us. At last a new day dawned, and we felt new confidence in our fellow creatures, and regretted that we had ever mistrusted them.

When they heard of our alarm I think, poor creatures, they felt it was only because they had been drinking and did not know what they were doing that we doubted them, for in their sober senses everyone showed us good feeling and respect, and people came from long distances to my dear mother for help when sick and in trouble, and she was always ready to do anything in her power for them. It comforted her in her sorrow to be of use to others. She was only thirty-three when my father died, and she returned a widow to the home they had built and beautified together, looking forward to many happy years. We left it for good not long after, as it was still quite too remote to be a suitable home for us. I should have mentioned that our overseer and his wife and young family lived quite near us. His house adjoined the store, and he had to remain there to protect it if necessary. Though the store had a lock our house had none; in the front French windows opened on to the veranda; the back door had a latch and a string. I believe there was a bolt, but it was seldom used, and I must say that except on that one occasion, when we gave way to quite unnecessary fears, we felt always strong in our weakness, and I am glad to say were quite justified in doing so.

When we left Glen Alice, Mr John Duncan, our good overseer, remained for a time to carry out the final arrangements and deliver the cattle and horses to their respective purchasers. The sheep were driven by my uncle's orders to a station of his at Beardi Plains, a long and weary journey. Our old shepherd, Taylor, was in charge, and such of our assigned servants as remained to us. The others had got or were entitled to their tickets-of-leave, and easily found employment with good wages. Glen Alice was let to Mr Russell for a time, then for a term of years to a company lately formed by Mr Benjamin Boyd. They added stabling and enclosures suitable for a depôt for horses, and finally the place was sold to Mr John Maclean, of Warrangee. I never saw it again, but my mother revisited it in 1848. I have a letter of hers describing her journey and her visit to Capita.

Chapter

4

PARRAMATTA INTERLUDE

I SHALL NOW pass on to the time we spent in Parramatta, where we lived from April 1841 till January 1843. Uncle Dalmahoy came to Capita for us, and we made one more long journey under his care. He had married Miss Goodsir the year before and settled in Parramatta, which was one of the reasons for our going there. My aunt was then in Sydney with her mother, so they kindly let us have their house for a month, that we might have time to look for a suitable home for ourselves.

The Parramatta races took place a few days after our arrival, and caused us much excitement, as we had never seen anything of the kind and were very fond of horses. We had an uninterrupted view of the racecourse, as there was only a piece of rough unenclosed ground between it and my uncle's house, and with the aid of a good telescope, or spy-glass as we then called it, we could quite well distinguish the different horses, and even some of the riders. Race cards had been given to us, and the horse we chose as our favourite was called Giggler, a very pretty creature. It did very well at first, but disappointed us greatly by bolting off the course, and so losing the race.

My mother finally decided on taking a cottage on the Western Road. It was then temporarily occupied by Mrs Bowerman and

"Port Macquarie in the 1830s" — *J. Backler*
(Hastings River Historical Society)

her family. She had let her beautiful place Mona, on the Parramatta river, and they were on the point of sailing for England. The chief attraction of this house was that it was near my uncle, and also near Madame Lubecki's school, which my sister and I were to attend. As winter advanced we found our cottage cold and damp; Margaret had a bad attack of rheumatic fever, while I had a cough and was obliged to give up my drawing lessons. I think we all missed the free and open-air life we had led at Glen Alice.

In the summer holidays my mother took us to visit her sister, Mrs Ogilvie, at Wallombi. We went by steamer to Morpeth, and drove from there. We enjoyed this change immensely, and quite recovered our health and spirits. My aunt had only one little girl, and it was then decided that they should come and visit us. Later on she joined my mother in taking Treganna House, in George Street. This was a large, commodious house with a good garden in front, and at one side, and a small green field at the back in which there were some pretty trees—among others two known as locust-trees. They had long pods full of beans which the Germans call *Johanes brodt,* and they certainly looked more suitable for food than live locusts, which some people suppose John the Baptist to have eaten.

Parramatta, though one of the oldest townships in the colony, was then very straggling and unformed. George Street extended from the Domain to the steamer wharf. The river was not navigable further up. The soldiers' barracks,[1] a huge brick building, stood near the wharf. The street consisted chiefly of dwelling-houses with gardens in front. On the north side was the old-fashioned inn known as the Red Cow, and long kept by Mrs Walker. It was apparently only a cottage in a garden, but, no doubt, was commodious and comfortable. Nearer Church Street were two good shops, originally dwelling-houses with deep verandas. One of these, called Nibblock and Tapps, was a general store, and very much frequented by us. I have still three very pretty little Worcester vases bought there.

[1] Designed by Francis Greenway: they are now demolished.

PARRAMATTA INTERLUDE

Nearer the Domain was Mrs Nash's Inn, more pretentious than its rival, the Red Cow. The coach for Sydney started from it, and there lived a tame magpie, a wonderful talker, well-known to all who entered the house. I was there several times when a child, and well remember how fascinated we were by it, though I suffered more than once from its vicious attacks. It had a horrible habit of hopping after children and pecking at their feet.

The band played sometimes in the Domain, but my mother did not often take us to hear it. I remember one day meeting a soldier's funeral, and, being very much impressed by the solemn music and the muffled drums, I felt quite shocked when, on their return from the cemetery, the same procession passed us marching gaily to a lively quick-step. We used very often to walk in the Government Domain. Not long after we settled in Parramatta there was a terrific storm, and the wind was quite alarming, sweeping all before it. Fortunately the area of its devastations was not very wide. We had a most interesting day in the Domain to see the traces that it had left. Our friend, Dr Bute Stewart, had arranged to meet there the Rev. Mr Clark, and Mr Dunlop, the astronomer, and he kindly invited us to join them with his daughter, who was taking out luncheon for the party. They had had a busy morning measuring trees and distances, and ascertaining all particulars of the storm. We often called on Mrs Dunlop at the Observatory. I do not remember how we became acquainted with her. She was a kindly woman; her husband, somewhat rough and coarse, but clever, and they were both very Scotch. Sir Thomas Brisbane was the means of establishing the Observatory in Parramatta, and of appointing Mr Dunlop.

There was no Presbyterian Church in Parramatta when we went there. The Rev. Mr Allan, the minister, held a service on Sunday morning in a private house, but it was not well attended, in fact there was not much room, and Mr Allan was far from eloquent, and could not carry on an extempore service. He afterwards joined the Episcopal Church. Mr Tait succeeded him. He was very popular, and a small temporary church was built near the river, which was largely attended.

Early in 1842 Uncle Arthur Ranken brought his family from the Lachlan to be near us, while he went again to Port Philip. Lorne, the fourth son, was born in March, and named after my mother. We were devoted to them all, and delighted when, later on, they joined us at Treganna House. George, the eldest, was a very stirring boy, and, though only four, was then sent to an infant school for two hours daily.

Much to our satisfaction, our uncle, Mr Macleod, took a house in Macquarie Street, and his family, scattered since their mother's death, re-assembled. We were very glad to see them all again and to renew our acquaintance with our two eldest cousins. They were delightful girls, and always very good to us. Our pleasant and intimate friends, the Patersons, were another large family. Mrs Paterson was a Miss MacLeod of Talisker. We all liked her very much. Three of the elder girls were at school with us at Madame Lubecki's.

I must say I enjoyed my time there, as I liked my lessons, and we had some very nice companions. Agnes Paterson was our particular friend; another was Charlotte Stewart, a very nice and clever girl. One of our friends rejoiced in the very peculiar

"The street consisted chiefly of dwelling-houses with gardens in front."

PARRAMATTA INTERLUDE

name of Hectorina. She was very pretty and amiable, and lived with a sister who was quite devoted to her and gave many little dances to amuse her and her young friends. I was sometimes allowed to join, and enjoyed myself very much. There was no lack of partners, as many of the young officers stationed at Parramatta enjoyed these informal little gatherings. Hectorina had many admirers among them, and was in despair when the regiment was ordered to India.

While we were still in our cottage on the Western Road our friends, Mr and Mrs Ranken, of Saltram, returned to the colony from Scotland. They had hurried back on account of the illness of their fourth son, and he, poor fellow, died on the voyage. They brought with them their two little boys, leaving three sons and four girls in Scotland for their education. Mrs Ranken came to see us, bringing with her Mr Hugh Hamilton, a young friend who had come from Ayrshire with them; I remember so well our disappointment that it was not one of her own boys, our former friends and playfellows. Had a glimpse into the future been given to us, we might have seen him twelve years later standing with Margaret in the old church as bride and bridegroom, myself as bridesmaid.

At the end of the year 1842 the rest of the Ranken family returned to Sydney. The climate of Scotland had proved too severe for the girls. Agnes died before they sailed, and Susan on the voyage. The others, with their governess, Miss Otto, spent a quiet Christmas with us before starting on their home-ward journey. I never saw Somervell (the eldest son) or the two girls again. Miss Otto went back to the Cape; the ship had put in there for a week on the voyage to Sydney, as was the custom at that time, and she had there met friends who induced her to return and settle there. Miss de Philipsthal then became their governess.

Just before Christmas my aunt, Mrs Ogilvie, met with rather an unpleasant adventure. She had occasion to visit her home at the Wollombi, and took the usual route by steamer to Morpeth, driving the rest of the journey. At that time gangs of bushrangers were out in various parts of the country, but she had no fear of meeting with any of them. The road was fairly good, though not much frequented. About noon they saw three men sitting by the roadside. As they approached, the men rose; one of them ordered the driver to stop, and then stood at the horse's head. The others stood at each side of the gig and demanded their money and valuables. My aunt had on a gold watch and chain, also several rings, all of which they took, except one ring that she managed to slip into her mouth. They did not interfere with her small amount of luggage and were quite cool, saying only to the driver as they were leaving, "Now, hurry up and don't look back."

The robbery was at once reported to the police. Some time afterwards Mrs Ogilvie got notice that they were in possession of a watch which answered the description of hers, and went to Sydney to claim it. She was then taken to Carter's Barracks,[1] where several prisoners were paraded before her, and she was asked if she had ever seen any of them before. She at once pointed out one as the man who had robbed her, and thought she recognized another. In both cases she was right, but fortunately had not to appear against them when they were tried. She got her watch back but nothing else, and much lamented the loss of an old and curious seal, which was a family treasure.

Chapter

5

AT LAKE INNES
1843

IN JANUARY 1843 we left Parramatta after a residence there of nearly two years, and went to Lake Innes, Port Macquarie, to visit my uncle and guardian, Major Innes, and to consult him as to our future plans; the result being that we remained at Lake Innes, which from that time became our home for some very happy years, and round which cling many fond memories, but we could not see into the future when somewhat reluctantly we again broke up our home and bade adieu to the many kind friends we then had in Parramatta.

On Thursday 26th, we went to Sydney, my mother, myself, and sister, and our faithful maid, Christina Ross. There was at that time a weekly steamer to Port Macquarie, and we expected to sail that evening. However, we found that the 26th, being the anniversary of the foundation of the Colony, on which day a great regatta always took place, our steamer had been engaged for some pleasure excursion, and the sailing delayed for twenty-four hours, so we enjoyed the sight of the regatta, and had an extra day in town. We left next night and stopped at Newcastle next morning to take in coal for the voyage, and landed for a short time, but looked with very little favour on our surroundings. In after years I thought it a very delightful place, and there spent more than ten of my happiest years.

Early on Sunday morning we sighted our port, and crossed the bar before ten o'clock. There was no one waiting to receive us, so we went to the hotel to await the arrival of the carriage, which we thought might be bringing some of the party from the Lake in time for church, but no one appearing, a messenger was sent off to tell of our arrival, and we, feeling rather sad and neglected, partook of some refreshment. As soon as possible a carriage dashed up to the door, driven by my uncle, who had come to meet us, and he explained that the steamer had passed unobserved by anyone at the Lake, so they were not expecting us when our messenger arrived.

In a few minutes we were comfortably seated in the carriage, and in an hour had stopped at the entrance gate, which was overhung by tall bamboos.[1] Here we alighted, as the large gate was rarely opened. The drive had cheered us, but a feeling of sadness lay beneath, and our dear mother, I am sure, recalled sorrowfully the day, nearly four years past, when we had all arrived there with my father, hoping that the change to a milder climate would restore his failing health. After four months of hopes and fears he was taken from us, and we went back to our home at Glen Alice in much sorrow; now we were returning to our kind friends at Lake Innes, and there was a prospect of our settling near them.

What a lovely afternoon that 29th of January was! There had been some rain in the early morning, and now as we walked up the wide approach the air was cool and fresh, laden with the sweet scent of roses and heliotrope, the leaves of the evergreens glittering in the sun, and a thousand gay flowers lending brightness to the scene. At the right hand the ground sloped away, and at the foot of the slope lay the lake, calm and bright in the glad sunshine. It was a lovely scene, and often as I have looked on it since with admiration, it never seemed fairer to me than it did on that day.

We were shown into the library, where my aunt received us most warmly, while presently Dido flew in and stood transfixed

[1] They are still there.

AT LAKE INNES (1843)

before us. She explained afterwards that she had expected to see two little girls, and when I, being five feet eight, stooped to kiss her, she felt inclined to cry with disappointment. She was then nearly eleven, but looked much older. Geordy was near eight, and Gustavus almost five. Two younger boys had died in infancy. St Clair was born in January 1840, and named after Aunt Barbara and Vivian.

When we left Parramatta it was with the idea of settling in a house of our own in or near Port Macquarie. We took all our furniture with us, or rather it followed in a sailing vessel, and on its arrival was stored till we required it, most of it for more than eight years, as it was soon decided that we should remain for some time at Lake Innes, my uncle and aunt making us welcome in the kindest manner. Aunt Barbara Innes had married my aunt's brother about two years before, and was still very much missed. My uncle was more than pleased that my mother should in some measure fill her place, as he liked having young people about him, and called us always his four girls.

During our long stay under his hospitable roof his kindness never flagged. He placed my mother at his left hand at table, saying, "Whoever may come to this house, remember that is to be always your place," and so it always was. I being very tall, was so far considered to be grown up that I dined at the late dinner, Margaret came to dessert with my cousins, and the four sat one at each side of my uncle and aunt. Dido was a tall girl for her age, in fact never grew any taller, and looked always as old as Margaret, who was nearly three years her senior. Gustavus was very devoted to his aunt Lorne, and to Margaret, calling the latter his fair cousin, and meaning it literally, as she had then a most fair and delicate complexion. Gordina was at once and always my especial friend. Margaret and Dido, being nearest in age though most unlike in everything else, agreed in being fast friends.

Shortly before our arrival their governess had left, and my aunt had herself undertaken the education of her girls, so her mornings were very fully and pleasantly occupied. In the after-

AT LAKE INNES (1843)

"Lake Innes" — *Dr George Herman Brujn*
(Hastings River Historical Society)

AT LAKE INNES (1843)

*The schoolroom—
no trifling or idle moments.*

noon she often rode, and the children walked with their maid, or they all drove to the beach. She also spent much time in the lovely gardens, where there was always something to plan or to superintend. She was an admirable housekeeper, and had many letters to write. There was a good library in the house, and a regular supply of books from the Sydney Library.

When it was settled that our stay should be indefinitely prolonged, my sister and I were included in the schoolroom party. I was then sixteen, and there I learned and said my lessons and did sums and translations in the good old-fashioned style for four years. We three elder girls worked together; no doubt I was in advance, but Dido was clever and ambitious, so we kept wonderfully together. My aunt was a strict disciplinarian, and as long as she lived I stood in awe of her.

She carried on the schoolroom work admirably, and allowed no trifling or idle moments. How she managed to devote the morning so entirely to us, having so many other claims on her attention, is now a mystery to me. We flew to the schoolroom at ten o'clock from the breakfast table; she followed in half an

hour and remained till one o'clock. We at once read together
the Psalms of the day, said texts, Collects, a hymn or portion of
Scripture; then followed quickly our various lessons, which
we had prepared before breakfast or the previous evening; then
we did sums for half an hour while she devoted herself to
Gustavus; after that we wrote to dictation, our interest in this
never flagging, and our anxiety about our mis-spells was never-
failing. I undertook to hear my youngest cousin practise daily
and to assist her with her lessons. She was a sweet child, and
developed into a charming woman. In the afternoon my mother
took us in hand, and worked, rode, or walked with us, so we
formed a very happy family party, and were quite independent
of interests or excitements from the outer world.

We were, however, very far from being dull or destitute of
amusement or society. There were gentlemen staying in the
house very often, but we seldom saw them except at dinner and
in the evening, and we never knew who might appear then,
as some rode out from Port Macquarie, others came from their
stations to spend a few days, or to await the arrival or departure
of the steamer, which for several years went regularly once a
week between Sydney and Port Macquarie, arriving at the latter
place early on Saturday morning and leaving on Monday as
the tide or bar suited. We got letters at that time only by the
steamer, but afterwards an overland mail was established, also
weekly, by Raymond Terrace and Manning River.

Since our visit to Lake Innes in 1839, the house had been
added to and the grounds enlarged, both being beautified in
many ways. The last addition comprised a large bedroom and
dressing-room, and over them the schoolroom and maid's-room.
My room opened from the schoolroom, and below it was the
china-room, which was entered from the back court, the whole
surmounted by a small square room which we called the "look-
out", as the upper half of each side was of glass, and each
afforded a wide view.

To the north one looked over the flower garden to a thickly
wooded and level tract of country, through which lay the road

to Port Macquarie; to the south, in the distance lay Camden Haven and the sea; to the east the hill between us and the sea, on which stood the flagstaff; to the west was the beautiful sun-lit lake, with lovely hills in the distance. The house now consisted of twenty-two apartments, all well and suitably furnished. This did not include bachelor's hall (a sitting-room and three good bedrooms), which opened into the garden and was quite separate. There some of the frequent visitors kept a supply of clothes; for others a good supply was kept by my always generous and lavish uncle, for he loved to keep open house and to share with others the good things that fortune had showered on him. In after days, when times had sadly changed, he often said, "I am no worse off than so-and-so, and look at the pleasure I have had, and have given to others, while he had neither."

One of my uncle's pleasures was to send a horse at once to any new arrival in the township, to be kept as long as they required it. This was really a boon to some of the young officers stationed at Port Macquarie, and much appreciated by them. Occasionally people rather imposed on his kindness. Once a man wrote and said the horse did not suit him, and described what he wanted, so, as horses were very plentiful, my uncle only laughed and sent another, but somehow the story got about.

The year 1840 was a time of unexampled prosperity in New South Wales. My uncle took a house in Sydney for the winter months. They had horses and carriages and a very large establishment, and were entertained by a large circle of friends, all of which they enjoyed to the full. At this time they bought many beautiful things, pictures, plate, etc., and a really magnificent set of Chinese china made to order, which comprised dinner and dessert, breakfast, tea and coffee sets, each complete, also hot water plates, and a set of three large and very beautiful bowls, with the Innes crest in colours on each. This china was very costly and was used only on special occasions.

I have by me a rough plan of the house and grounds, stables and outbuildings, which gives some idea of their size and extent. There was a wide double veranda to the front of the house, which faced the Lake and the setting sun. A veranda extended along the whole of the south side. The drawing-room was a large square room at the corner, 20ft by 24ft, with two French windows to the west, and two to the south, opening on to the veranda. It was upholstered in yellow satin damask. Between the windows to the west stood a cabinet and tall handsome mirror; opposite was the fireplace, above which was another mirror.

Between the south windows hung a very fine picture by Paul Veronese, representing Achilles when in hiding at the Court of King Lycomedes, and dressed as a girl, betraying himself to Ulysses, disguised as a pedlar, by drawing his sword. I remember a stranger who had travelled a great deal in Italy standing amazed before it the first time he entered the room, and exclaiming, "What, a Paulo, and here!" He supposed he had arrived at the end of the earth or of civilization. There were other good pictures in the house—one in the dining-room had a musical box concealed in a somewhat clumsy frame; in the library there were some family pictures, none of them large or remarkable; a pretty picture of my grandmother Innes in water colours, my uncle and three of his brothers in oils, and some others. There were three large bookshelves from the floor to the ceiling filled with many choice books.

When we went to Port Innes in 1843 times had changed, and the Colony was in a very depressed state, so the establishment at Lake Innes had been very much reduced. Everything seemed to us very luxurious, but we were told that nearly half the servants had been dismissed. There was still a butler and two footmen, a piper, who assisted when wanted, and two Spaniards who were attached to the stables, but appeared in livery at times. They looked very smart, and waited well. My aunt had a maid (the butler's wife), and my cousins had a nice Highland maid who came to the Colony in the same ship with our maid, Christina Ross, and afterwards married the piper. There were also two housemaids and a laundress. All the years we were at the Lake my aunt and we four girls all wore white dresses, which entailed a good deal of work, but if the climate made it almost necessary it also favoured the laundress; we wore alpaca or fine merino in winter, changing invariably on the 14th May and 15th October.

Among our most favourite and frequent visitors were the Messrs James, Patrick, and Hugh Mackay, who lived about twenty miles inland on the way to New England, at a place they called Big House, after their old paternal home in Sutherlandshire. With them for a time lived their cousins, Messrs William and Gerard Robertson. Mr Patrick Mackay arrived in the Colony in 1839, and Mr James Mackay came to Port Macquarie in January 1843, only the week before we did. Mr Robert Graham was an older resident, and we used to see him at Lake Innes when we were there in 1839, and admired him at a humble distance. Mr William M'Kenzie, afterwards Sir William M'Kenzie of Coul, and he were partners, and called their place on the Maria River Coulfintray, a name provocative of many weak jokes in our almost tropical climate.

Mr Gray, the Police Magistrate, lived in Port Macquarie, and Mr Robert Massie, C.C.L. for the Macleay, was often with him, and they generally rode out together to dinner. There was a military officer stationed at Port Macquarie and a resident Commissariat Officer, also a Colonial surgeon. The clergyman was a Colonial chaplain appointed by Government, the district being still a depôt for invalids, and a chain gang at work at the dam completing the road to New England.[1] It was hoped that Port Macquarie would become the established port for the shipment of wool, etc., to Sydney, and that the drays from New England would from there take back the necessary supplies to the stations. As time went on these hopes were doomed to disappointment, as transportation ceased, and Government gradually withdrew its support from the district, the invalids died off, and the road to New England was finished. It never was a good road, and there were no men available for keeping it in repair.

To crown all, the bar gradually became almost impassable, so the traffic from New England was diverted to Morpeth and Newcastle, and Port Macquarie sunk into comparative insignificance.

In March 1843 a splendid Comet appeared and was visible for about three weeks. We saw it first on Friday, 3rd, at about six o'clock. We had just returned from a long day at the beach when we were called to the front of the house to see a wonderful appearance in the sky. Looking due west over the lake we beheld a really splendid Comet. It disappeared in about two hours, following as it were the setting sun. I give the following particulars from a journal kept at the time:

Saturday, 4th March 1843. This has been a beautiful, bright, clear day. In the evening we all watched anxiously for the Comet. It appeared before seven o'clock, at first faintly, but as the night became darker we saw it distinctly. It is indeed magnificent. The tail looked even longer than it did last night. The star to which the tail is attached is small, that is to say it does not appear to us larger than the other stars or brighter, but the tail is beautiful, springing upwards from the star like an aigrette of light. We thought the whole length of the Comet, when the star reached the horizon, was half the distance to the Zenith, and the breadth of the tail at the widest part one fourth of its length. Last night there was a long thin streak of light from the tail which looked like a continuance of it, though it came from one side only, and in a slanting direction.

Monday, 6th March. The Comet not so bright, owing I suppose to the moon being older and the light from it stronger.

Wednesday, 8th March. Saw the Comet very distinctly. The tail was visible long after the star had disappeared. The weather is still very fine.

Friday 10th March. Extremely warm all day. We hear that some of the people in Port Macquarie firmly believe that the world is coming to an end, and say it was prophesied a hundred years ago that a Comet would appear in 1843 which would

---

[1] The prisoners were housed in large brick barracks and a jail. Only the foundations of the jail remain.

destroy the world. This sounds very alarming, but we heard nothing about it till the Comet appeared, and now it is easy for anyone to prophesy. We half hoped the Comet would not be seen tonight, for though it is very beautiful and we have a certain amount of pleasure in looking at it, we have also an indescribable dread of it. There was a great deal of lightning tonight, and some heavy clouds.

Saturday, 11th March. Got up early to gather flowers. The heat was dreadful. After breakfast it increased so much we began to think there must be some truth in the report that the Comet is to burn us up. When my aunt came to the schoolroom she told us a great deal about comets, and said that though this one may possibly be the cause of the great heat, there is no danger of the world being destroyed by it. People had often before imagined the end of the world was at hand, but of that day and hour no man knoweth. We saw the Comet again tonight: it is very splendid. It appears later every evening and is longer visible and higher up. The tail seems longer and thinner, but is still bright and beautiful, though the moonlight just now partially eclipses it.

Monday, 13th March. A lovely morning and tolerably cool. We quite enjoyed it. I cannot help feeling silly about the Comet. We saw it again tonight, but it does not now look so large and bright as at first.

Tuesday till Friday it rained almost continuously, so we did not see the Comet. The journal continues:

Saturday, 18th March. When I awoke this morning I was delighted to see the sun shining as if there had never been a cloud. We saw the Comet, though very faintly. It was higher than usual, and if we had not known where it was likely to appear and looked particularly for it, I do not think we should have discovered it.

Sunday, 19th March. We went out after dinner to see if the Comet was still visible and were much surprised to see it

distinctly (the moon had not risen). There were two streamers
of light from it which we had never observed before, the one
on our left as we stood opposite to it seemed to come from the
star, the other on the right from the tail and much higher up.
They were in a circular form and soon became indistinct. The
star was sometimes very bright. We also saw the stars through
the upper part of the tail of the Comet.

Tuesday, 21st March. Saw the Comet this evening. It was very
faint.

Friday, 24th March. Saw the Comet, and observed stars distinctly through the tail.

After this the Comet is not mentioned again in my journal.

In June 1843 the election of members took place for the first
Legislative Assembly in the Colonies. Queensland was then part
of New South Wales, and Victoria also sent representatives,
but at the time our interest centred entirely in the fact that my

"*. . . a lovely morning
and tolerably cool.*"

AT LAKE INNES (1843)

aunt's father, Mr Alex. Macleay, late Colonial Secretary, was one of the candidates for the counties in which Port Macquarie was included, and was coming to meet and address the electors. All was pleasureable excitement and expectation. My uncle went up to Sydney to be his escort, and they were expected to arrive on the morning of the 17th.

Unfortunately, the weather was very bad. They had a long and stormy passage, arrived late, and found the bar impassable and the boat harbour unsafe. They lay off the port all night, and finally a few of the passengers, including my uncle and Mr Macleay, were landed early next morning. The boat narrowly escaped being swamped, while the steamer had to take refuge at Trial Bay. The weather all night was wild and stormy, the waves rolling heavily on the beach, making a tremendous roar. In the morning we could see that at Camden Haven the headland was crowned with white foam, which dashed incessantly against it. My aunt had had a wakeful and anxious night, and we were all in a state of great excitement when a messenger arrived to say that all was well and the carriage approaching. The travellers were most warmly welcomed, and looked nothing the worse of their rough voyage. Mr Macleay was just as I remembered him nine years before, when I was a little school girl at Sydney. Mr Gray and Colonel Gordon dined with us; the latter came down in the steamer and landed with my uncle. He is in the Engineers, and came to Sydney quite lately as successor to Colonel Barney.[1]

I shall now give some extracts from an old journal kept at the time:

Monday, 19th June. When we went down this morning, Bruce was in the veranda playing a grand pibroch. Mr Macleay is delighted with the bagpipes; he speaks Gaelic quite well, and so does Colonel Gordon. The gentlemen went to the settlement and did not return till late. In the evening there was a dinner

---

[1] Lieut.-Colonel James Gordon in 1842 somewhat curiously applied for the position of Chief Engineer in Sydney while Lieut.-Colonel George Barney was occupying the position. Gordon's application was refused by the Governor in January 1843.

party, eight gentlemen besides the four in the house, my aunt, and mamma.

Tuesday, 20th June. I was scarcely awake when Bruce began to play under Mr Macleay's windows, and we had the full benefit of "Johnnie Cope" and some fine pibrochs. Afterwards he played in the veranda, the gentlemen quite enjoying it. In the afternoon my uncle, aunt, and Gustavus drove to the beach with Mr Macleay. I went off to gather flowers, as I had offered to fill the large epergne as a special decoration for the dinner table. I had no idea of the difficulty of the undertaking, but, with Jane's assistance, succeeded very well. She got me some fine hollyhocks from the new garden, about two feet high, which formed the centre. The large crystal bowl was filled with fine white salt, and the stems of the flowers supported in it; when all was completed I saw it placed on the dinner table with not a little complacency. There was again a large dinner party, and after-dinner speeches with much cheering, followed by music and dancing, in which Mr Macleay, and my aunt, my uncle, and my mother joined. I had never seen mamma dance before, though she often sings while she teaches us some reel steps. Mr Macleay showed us an old country dance called "The Country Bumpkin" which amused us very much. I cannot give a very instructive description of it, but it is danced by six ladies and six gentlemen, the gentleman in the centre of the circle wearing a hat which he puts on one of the others, who then takes his place, and so on. I danced with Mr Salwey, who is most amusing. He had never seen the Highland dress till this evening. After looking at Bruce for some time, he asked if it was not very unusual to wear top boots when in full dress! I must explain that he is very short sighted. Colonel Gray, Capt. Gordon, R.N., Capt. Jobling, Dr Carlyle, Mr Acroyd, Mr Evans, Mr Gray, Mr Salwey, and Dr Richardson were of the party.

Wednesday, 21st June. Was again awakened by the sound of the bagpipes. The gentlemen went to Port Macquarie to attend a lunch given by Mr Macleay. We went up the hill to enjoy the fine view and fresh air, after the fatigues of the night before. The burning of fallen trees is getting on splendidly and is a great improvement. Margaret and I dined to make up the party, as some of the expected guests did not arrive. It was my first dinner party, and I quite enjoyed it. Capt. Wauch, Capt. Jobling, Mr Montgomerie, and Mr Purves were among the guests. After they had gone, Capt. Gordon proposed dancing "Shawntrews" but as he could only dance it to a tune which no one could play, the dance was given up, and Bruce danced "Gillie Callum" over the poker and tongs crossed on the floor, instead of over drawn swords. Mamma sang, and we all kept time. We were quite delighted, and Bruce danced so well and lightly.

Thursday, 22nd June. The weather continues as fine as could possibly be wished for. Bruce played some pibrochs early for Mr Macleay's benefit. I had no idea the bagpipes could sound so beautiful, though I liked them at all times, but the sound is quite different in the open-air, when the piper is walking up and down, and the drone, that I hated above all things, is swelling and sinking so grandly. I quite wonder now that when I first heard them I thought the sound so dreadful and uncouth. After lunch we went to the garden for flowers to fill the epergne very splendidly, as there was a large party expected. Mamma brought some beautiful evergreens from the back of the hill. My aunt asked us if we had pink sashes, as pink was her father's colour, and she wished us very much to wear pink. Margaret had one but I had not, so was going to wear white, when my aunt brought me a very handsome pink satin one which I joyfully accepted, and we four girls appeared very gaily, to the envy of the gentlemen, who begged for a bow to wear tomorrow. Mr Graham, Capt. Gordon, Capt. Wauch and others dined here. Mr Gray returned to his never-ending subject of Highlanders, declaring he was half a Highlander himself. I looked incredulous, upon which he assured me that ladies should not believe what gentlemen say to them. I at once agreed that I could not believe that he was even half a Highlandman, and he got so excited about it that I thought in a short time he would have convinced himself that he had been born and bred, and perhaps was still living, in the Highlands. We had no dancing this evening, and retired early to make up favours to be worn at the election to-morrow. My aunt provided us with a roll of pink ribbon and a pattern, and we worked away very merrily. I made one for Mr Macleay of which I felt very proud, and Dido made one for her papa. All the others were marked for our mutual friends, not forgetting one for Pine. My aunt came in several times while we were working, bringing first materials, then biscuits and hot wine and water, but her last visit tended more to the amusement of the party, she being the bearer of a letter for Christina which contained a proposal, couched in the most condescending terms, and concluding with, "Your loving husband that is to be". I only make so free with it as we think it was written to tease her, though in truth she has no lack of admirers and proposals. I must now say something of the dinner party today, though rather late. The table presented a splendid appearance, being laid very handsomely for eighteen persons. The epergne was quite beautiful, and when placed in the centre of the table the flowers were as high as the lamp. I must own I was rather glad when it was removed. There were two silver wine coolers with light wines, and branch candlesticks with wax candles, and four silver side dishes: we had two soups and an immense variety of dishes. Bruce and the butler waited, and we had four footmen in livery. I felt quite dazzled, as I had never been at so splendid an entertainment before.

Friday, 23rd June. This eventful morning dawned with all the brightness of the finest spring day. We all rose early, roused by the strains of the bagpipes. We had a great discussion as to how the pipes should be decorated for the day's performance, as all the pink ribbon had been used up except a few scraps saved from the horses' favours. I think it wonderful there was so much, as it was by mere chance that my uncle named that colour, the important matter being quite forgotten till yesterday in the novelty of the election, though he was then told that one of the long-sighted ladies in Port Macquarie had seen Mr Macleay's colours flying on board the steamer when she arrived. We all appeared with great pink bows and favours, which were distributed to the gentlemen present, and the rest sent to Port Macquarie, for which place they all set off immediately after breakfast—Mr Macleay, my uncle, and Captain Gordon in the close carriage, the other gentlemen on horseback. We afterwards heard that they had not gone far when they were joined by six horsemen bearing flags, who rode before them all the rest of the way. We went to the front gate to see their departure, and found there an admiring crowd of natives profusely decorated with pink calico, which looked very gay. One man had a long streamer tied to the end of the tuft of grass on which they roll their hair, and which floated from it gracefully in the breeze. Upon our return to the house we set to work busily to dismantle the pink room. It has been arranged that the steamer is not to leave till tomorrow evening, and there is to be in the morning here a cold luncheon in honour of Mr Macleay's eightieth birthday, which by a happy coincidence will be tomorrow. A large party is expected, and tables are to be laid in two rooms. Margaret and Dido undertook the decoration of the pink room after the bed had been taken down and the furniture removed. It really is a very pretty room, with a half glass door opening on to the veranda. One of the windows looks out upon the prettiest part of the garden, the other into the back veranda and back court. The blind of this window is to be pinned over with pink roses, which will have a very pretty effect, and prevent inquisitive people from attempting to lift it. After lunch we went up the hill, intending to finish burning the tree, as there was so little left, but found that we could not do it without assistance, so we invited one of our countrymen to our aid, as there was a small party encamped quite near. Two gentlemen and a lady presently appeared, and under our able superintendence soon made up a very respectable fire. When we returned we found the gardener busy ornamenting the rooms with

AT LAKE INNES (1843)

beautiful evergreens; mamma had been out with Geordy and Tay in search of them.

Saturday, 24th June. I got up as soon as I could see, but as the morning was very dark found to my horror it was nearly seven o'clock. We all hastened to the garden where we at once commenced operations by attacking all the China rose bushes within our reach, and robbing them of their gay bloom. The ornamenting of the breakfast table had been entrusted to me, so I provided myself with a large quantity of the choicest roses, and filled a number of champagne glasses and other glasses with them, and stole from the gardener some of his choicest buds; he had just come in, steps in hand, to put fresh flowers among the evergreens, as pink is to be the prevailing colour. It was a most fortunate choice, as pink roses are so abundant. When I had filled the epergne, which looked exceedingly pretty, I went to see how the good people in the other rooms were getting on. Mamma had joined them, and was making a wreath to ornament the library mirror. Dido was busy pinning roses on the blind, Margaret arranging them in the fireplace, Gordina bustling about in everyone's way, and Gustavus trying to sweep away the fallen leaves, Mr Mackay and Mr Robertson looking on complacently.

Once more we went to the garden and again returned laden with the chosen flowers, some of which we placed on the breakfast plates, and when my aunt came down she said everything looked extremely well. My mother had decorated the library and made some beautiful wreaths, one of which was hung over Mr Macleay's picture, with which he was well pleased, as well as with the quantity of his chosen colour displayed upon the breakfast table. After breakfast I got the steps and adorned the chandelier in the drawing-room. Some more roses being still required for the vases, we went in search of them, fearing there might not be even one left, but to our surprise there were still plenty, and had I not known of the quantities that had been gathered I would scarcely have missed them. All being in readiness, I thought I would go quietly to the schoolroom and finish my letters before the arrival of the guests, but had scarcely collected my scattered ideas when I was called down again. There was a host of people in the veranda, and in the drawing-room were Captain Geary and Mr G——, the latter a strange-looking person who appeared to be keeping strict guard over a hideous hat. When Mr Montgomerie appeared he was most indignant that no favour had been ticketed for him. I tried in vain to apologize for the mistake, which I could not account for. At last mamma kindly gave him hers, and Dido pinned it on, and he was restored to smiles and happiness. The procession to luncheon soon after commenced. My uncle said that we cousins had better go to his office, which adjoins the pink room, where Mr Mackay was to preside, and that a small table was ready for us: there we feasted right merrily till a loud and long "hip, hip, hurrah" from the next room, responded to by one from the dining-room, warned us it was time for us to retire. We met Mr M'Kenzie, who had made his escape, and was anxious to return at once to Port Macquarie to his friend and partner, Mr Graham, who had met with an accident and so been unable to join the party. Lunch in both rooms went off with great éclat, and then the whole party went out to the lawn. When we went down again we found about twenty natives assembled there and dancing vigorously, while Bruce played. When they had finished, Dido proposed that we should dance a reel, and at once the whole party seemed inspired with a wish to join, and really there could not have been a gayer scene; we four girls in white frocks and pink sashes and bows flying through the dance pursued by nimble partners, mine a gentleman in green whose name I do not even know, occupied one end of the veranda, the rest being crowded with onlookers who had not been happy enough to find partners, while another party, all gentlemen, danced upon the lawn.

The natives who had before been figuring there now lay upon the grass and looked on with admiring eyes. Bruce marched about in his Highland dress, his bagpipes decorated with a pink scarf besides its tartan ribbons. The veranda posts were also gay with streamers, some of which had mottoes printed on them, such as "Macleay for ever". But now the merry scene is at an end, the carriage is approaching, the music stops, my green partner makes a profound bow, and in a moment all appears confusion, all are intent on securing their hats, their coats, their gigs, their horses, and such shaking of hands, such cordial goodbyes. The six flag-bearers advanced and seized their colours, and in a few minutes more all were in readiness to start, and the carriage door was shut and the horsemen mounted. Bruce was in one of the gigs, but minus his pipes, which Capt. Gordon flourished triumphantly aloft. All the horsemen but four rode two and two in advance of the carriages, some carrying flags. One of the gigs also went before, while the others and two riders followed, and the other two rode on each side. In this order they marched through Port Macquarie, and by that time Bruce had regained his pipes and played his best and liveliest.

Well, all the good people having departed, we took a parting look round the deserted rooms, which presented a miserable contrast to the freshness and beauty of the morning; then we changed our dresses and went out for a walk, and to visit our fires on the hill. In the evening the servants had a dance and supper in the hall, and so ended this gay and eventful week—assuredly the most lively that I have ever spent.

Monday was such a lovely day, we had good hopes that the steamer had had a return passage good enough to make up for her stormy passage down. Mr P. and Mr H. Mackay left. In the afternoon we walked to the beach and had a most delightful bathe in the sea, and afterwards gathered some pretty shells. Mr Gunn, who we call Pine, otherwise the friend of the family, came out to dinner. I discovered what I thought was a brown ball in one of the high branches of the Norfolk Island pine-trees. My aunt said it was a seed cone, so Mr Patrick positively exerted himself so far as to ascend and bring it down, though not without breaking the pretty way in which it grew. A greener one was discovered which Mr Hugh determined to try for, as my aunt was anxious to get a perfect one. He is very tall, and of course heavy, so I really feared that the slender branches would give way with him, but with his brother's help and mamma's parasol they succeeded in getting it off. It is very pretty, and marked much like a pineapple and has a very resinous smell.

30th June. The fine weather still continues; the steamer landed a mail this morning, and went on to the Clarence. My aunt heard of her father's safe arrival in Sydney, quite well after all his fatigue here, and delighted with Port Macquarie and his visit to her. Of course nothing is talked of but the elections, and the different parties likely to be returned to represent the country in the new Legislative Assembly. I may here say that Mr Macleay was elected for Port Macquarie, and was afterwards the first Speaker of the Legislative Council.

After the election we had a very quiet time, and during the rest of the winter and spring took many delightful walks, thus acquainting ourselves as far as possible with our immediate surroundings, selecting sheltered spots in which to hold our birthday picnics, and noting the places in which the wild raspberries and Cape gooseberries grew most abundantly. Our favourite walk then and always was to the beach, about two miles from the house. There we often bathed or gathered shells and seaweed, or dug for cockles, which sometimes we carried home and had cooked for the schoolroom tea—tough morsels and indigestible, but that in no way interfered with our love for them.

The poultry yard and "cultivation", a sort of home farm, was situated about half way to the beach, and bounded on two sides by the marshy ground at the end of the lake, which sometimes flowed from Cati[1] Creek into the sea. This marsh extended also for some distance north at the back of the hill, on the west side of which the house was built. A sandy flat lay between the swamp and the sea.

[1] Now Cathie Creek.

At the poultry yard were two cottages built on a piece of rising ground, one for the men who worked in the fields, the other for the Halorans'. There were pig-sties and sheds for the poultry, but I must own both pigs and fowls enjoyed a good deal of freedom. Haloran was a quiet, elderly Irishman, he had been one of my father's assigned servants, and left Capita with our sheep. I don't quite know how his wife found her way to the colony, but there she was, and a decent, industrious creature, more than content to find herself so comfortably provided for, and quite happy among pigs and fowls, or as she herself called them, "The pigs and the rest of the poulthry". In the fields grew oats and lucerne for hay, also maize and Indian corn, Bruce having the charge or oversight of all. After passing the cottages we went through a gate, and almost immediately entered on a kind of bridge or roadway made on wooden piles. This road was formed during the early days of convict labour, when Port Macquarie was for a time a penal settlement and there was very little work for the men to do. The bridge extended for quite a quarter of a mile through a marshy swamp, then we got on to a sandy road raised above the surrounding damp flat. A broad, deep ditch had been cut at each side, and the soil thrown on to the roadway. The ditches were often quite full of water, and the road generally very damp; being white sand and full of small roots, it was never dusty. The sandy flat extended to the sea, and in spring and summer was gay with lovely flowers of many kinds; we often crossed the ditches and gathered as many as we could carry. In December it was always full of magnificent Blandfordias.

28th October 1843. My uncle arrived from Sydney, bringing with him Captain Hemry and Mr Heale. The former was very kind to the little Laurentz Campbells when taking them home from the Cape some years ago. The latter has been a great traveller, and is most conversational, telling us of many of the interesting places he had visited in Europe, South America, the East and West Indies, and New Zealand. He spoke of the

" . . . selecting sheltered spots
in which to hold our birthday picnics."

AT LAKE INNES (1843)

murder of the English settlers there a short time ago. Everyone seems to agree in saying that they were the aggressors, but blame the natives for killing them after they had surrendered. I was happy to hear Mr Heale's praises of Sydney and its beautiful harbour. It is wonderful to think that less than sixty years ago there was not a European in the country—and now! but why boast? As both the gentlemen wished to see something of this part of the Colony, my uncle has kindly arranged to take them to Yarrows and to Tilbuster.

31st October being Hallowe'en, before going to bed we young people assembled in the old nursery to have our fortunes told, and found Helen with eggs, water and glasses, prepared to read the fates of all who came to her. Her own had been told before we came into the room; of course the bagpipes were there, to say nothing of the piper. We began by each taking a wine-glass and half-filling it with clear water, then we dropped into it part of the white of an egg. The fortune-teller is then supposed to see in the glass any initials that may be appropriate, besides other remarkable objects, such as a church or a ship. In my glass various letters were said to be seen very distinctly so [sic] I felt no interest in any of them. Margaret followed with two; Dido had none given; it was not necessary. Then we all set off to the new garden to pull up cabbage stocks, and returned in triumph with very straight and flourishing specimens, mine certainly the largest. We then got each a piece of shortbread into which a ring had been baked. Helen's piece contained the ring, so she of all the party is to be married first (and so she was). On this occasion we did not "duck for apples"; we did not learn till afterwards of the modern and more agreeable plan of dropping a fork into one of the floating apples. Next morning we searched for the slips of paper we had buried in the lawn, each with a name written on it, but alas! only one was to be found, and everyone but the fortunate finder was inconsolable.

7th November. Got up very early to finish a pair of cuffs I have been working as a birthday gift for mamma. There is a most beautiful cactus in flower at the pink room window, the outside a brilliant crimson, but I do not know of any colour so lovely as the centre; it is so bright and soft and beautiful, with a kind of purple bloom over it. The new swarm of bees has already half-filled its box with beautiful white wax. One pursued Dido, who made her escape, but it stung Margaret. They never interfere with me. I gathered some ripe strawberries for my uncle.

On Sunday 13th our visitors left after an early breakfast. The steamer from Clarence waited off the bar for them, and we all felt quite sorry to say goodbye, probably never to meet again. They had visited Yarrows and Rolands Plains with my uncle, and we had taken them to the beach, but the most delightful and unexpected treat to us was that we all went out more than once on the lake. The boats were kept generally under water, but one was soon raised and got ready; we stepped gaily in, and the gentlemen pushed off. The boat glided gently through the tall rushes into the open lake; it was a most delightful afternoon—the sun shining brightly and the wind cool and refreshing, scarcely a ripple on the smooth surface of the water, on which we saw multitudes of wild ducks swimming and diving for their food. They were very tame, and allowed us to approach quite near.

We also saw some black swans sailing gracefully about; they, however, soon spoiled their appearance by taking flight. The air is certainly not their element, for they stretch out their long necks and flap their wings, allowing the white feathers under them to be seen. We were not very successful in our fishing, though we saw some fine fish jumping among the reeds; one odd looking little thing we got was called a cat fish. We sailed almost round the lake, which looks much larger when one is on it than it does from the land: then we "hove to" in a little bay, where the lines were again thrown out to fish, and we all tried to throw out lines of another description. Mr Heale told us of an amusing game called "bout-rimer". One of the party gives out two or four words that rhyme, from which every one present is expected to make a verse, each line ending with one of the words given. We were not at all equal to the occasion, though the words seemed easy enough, being clime, time, flower, bower. This is the only one I remember, and will serve as an example:

> In fair Australia's sunny clime,
> The morn we rove 'mid shrub and flower,
> At eve we dance in lady's bower,
> Gaily and swiftly flies the time . . .

and with us it passed merrily till it was time to leave. After dinner, of course, we danced and found ourselves quite perfect in Sir Roger de Coverley, which Captain Hemry had taught us. We kept it up for an hour with unabated spirit. I wondered at Bruce going on for so long with apparent ease. He played "The Flowers of Edinburgh", not knowing the correct time, but I have had a hunt through an old book of reels and found "The Haymakers", which is the same thing, and he is to learn it. The steamer not appearing on Saturday as expected gave us time for another delightful sail on the lake, and a most amusing afternoon in the library, where Mr Wemyss recited "Young Lochinvar" while Mr Heale furnished the action. The arrangement is that the person reciting stands with his hands behind his back, and someone standing behind him thrusts his hands forward instead. When Mr Heale recited the opening speech in *Richard the Third*, "Now is the winter of our discontent", Captain Hendry acted remarkably well; he pulled down his waistcoat, adjusted the collar of his coat, buttoned it up, then threw it open, and finally took out his handkerchief and wiped his forehead. It was most cleverly done by both, and really very absurd and amusing.

We had another attempt at bout-rimer, without much success, but that it amused some of the party. The following was the best effort.

To the Temple of Parnassus I shall never climb,
    For the verses I write are all wanting in feet;
I wish I could write what would last for all time,
    And leave to mankind a memorial sweet.

About this time some of my former love for drawing began to revive, and Dido and I resolved to paint at least one wild flower every week, beginning with the charming little blue commelina. We collected flowers and berries of every description. Mr Hugh Mackay brought us some of the large purple fruit that grows near Bighouse. It is called by some people the "native fig", not from any resemblance it bears to that fruit, for it is much larger and is more the shape of an apple or plum, and has three long hard seeds embedded in the pulp. It certainly is very pretty; the skin is very thin and of a bright rich purple colour, something like a large purple plum. They require to be kept till they are soft, when the skin peels easily off. The fruit itself is of a yellowish colour, streaked with pink. I thought it rather good, but dry, and with the slightly resinous flavour common to all the native fruits. I had no idea till now that there was any so large. The trees, I believe, are loaded with them, and the leaf is dark and glossy.

On St Andrew's day we five cousins and Mr Mackay walked to the poultry-yard, the whole family—ducks, geese, pigs, chickens, and baby—were flourishing, and did Mrs Haloran credit, but she complained sadly of the young turkeys dying. "Sure it breaks my heart entirely to see them dhropping off, and me rare-ing them so noice." The last time we walked down she was very long in coming to open the gate for us. We managed to open it ourselves, and mamma said to her: "You see you were not smart enough." "'Deed, ma'am, and that's the truth, and that's what was keeping me back, thinking if I could come in these rags," (displaying a robe of faded yellow, much torn, and bare feet) adding, she always wore her wedding shoes and stockings.

We were then on our way to the beach to bathe, and before we entered the water mamma gave a ring she was wearing to

Jane to keep for her, and Jane put it into Gustavus's shoes. When we were nearly dressed she asked if anyone had taken the ring, but no one had seen it. In vain we searched, crawling carefully over the sand where we had been. Our fear then was that it had fallen into the sea, where Jane was dipping and wringing our bathing dresses, when she remembered about it. At last we gave up all hope of finding it, and returned home. Next morning, on entering mamma's room, the first thing I saw was the ring. How delighted I was. Lahye (the butler) had gone to the beach very early with Jane and Christina, and had sifted the dry sand where we had been standing, having first drawn a circle round the spot, and was fortunate in finding it. Happily, the tide had been very low during the night with no wind to drift the sand.

Mr Mackay showed us a stockwhip, which he is going to send to Scotland. After displaying his own talents in cracking it, he asked if I would try. It was by no means the first time I had handled a stockwhip, and I rather astonished him by the masterly manner in which I cracked it.

We have been much amused at hearing of the golden idea which some people "at home" entertain of Australia. Two gentlemen who arrived in the Colony early this year said to my aunt the other day, "It is no wonder we are disgusted with the country. We thought we had only to pick up money, it increased so fast, and without troubles or annoyances." They explained that their cousin, who came out before they did, was expected to write at once and tell them what he thought of this fine country. As he did not do so, out came his brother to share in his supposed good fortune, but still they sent no word home. "Come," thought the other two—"They shall not keep all those good things to themselves, no doubt they are quietly picking up the guineas, we had better lose no more time." I wonder if they thought they had found a goldmine, with a mint complete, concealed of course, but sending forth a golden harvest in showers. Well, one left a merchant's office in which he had every prospects of becoming a partner. The other had

AT LAKE INNES (1843)

just become a W.S. in Edinburgh. Both determined to start off at once to Sydney, and astonish their friends by their brilliant success. But lo, they were met by the cry of "bad times". All the guineas had disappeared, if there had ever been any! What was to be done? They could not go back, so, to make the best of a bad job, they have lowered their ideas so far as to become "settlers" (wretched word) and deferred the pleasures of gathering guineas till they have worked for and deserved them. "Bad times" is at present the too general subject of conversation; everyone takes an interest in it, and it is melancholy to hear of the number of people who are absolutely in want of the necessaries of life, who lately were in affluence. No one seems to have an idea as to how it will all end.

16th December. I have been devoting a great deal of time to my friends lately, and had twelve letters ready when we were told the parcel was not to be sent for a week. My uncle returned from Sydney on the 2nd and went off again on the 11th. Meantime we have had a great many people coming and going —Mr Wemyss, Mr Graham, the Messrs Mackay, Mr William Robertson (who insists on helping up to "pluck" flowers every morning), Mr Gray, Mr M'Lean, and a Mr Watertson [*sic*], who came out to dinner. We have danced nearly every evening. Gustavus now dances very well, and his kilt is very becoming. Bruce has made him a sporran, of which he is quite proud. My uncle calls him "Young Lochinvar", but that it quite wrong, as that gallant young knight was certainly a Lowlander.

We make pleasant raids into the new garden every afternoon. The first ripe figs were gathered on the 6th, but now there are Chinese peaches and mulberries, as well as quantities of figs. I cannot say I like the flavour of these double blossomed peaches. The Moreton Bay chestnut is now in flower, of a scarlet and yellow colour, and grows in clusters on the bare branches without leaves near them.

We all love our morning in the schoolroom, and have got a new geographical lesson to prepare for Saturday. Instead of drawing names of places from a bag and merely telling their whereabouts, we each get three names given to us on Monday, and on Thursday give some interesting information about each place, and get new ones to prepare for the following Monday. My first were rather varied—Ramillies, New York, Vittoria. I liked the next week better, Jamaica having fallen to my lot. I think I shall have to look into *Tom Cringle's Log* for a description of some of its glories. Our dictation just now is about Sir Roger de Coverley. We begged for it, as we all like the country dance of the name; of course, we like Sir Roger himself, and have a particular regard for his ancestor, who was said to have been the first to introduce the fashion of making love by squeezing the hand—I was going to add, I wish he had left it alone.

I must say something here about Gustavus's tortoise, which he is devoted to, but I think the poor creature leads a wretched life. He has now got a string fastened to its shell, and it is fastened to a tree. If it tries to make a hole for itself in the soft earth it is pulled out at once in case it should be choked. Then water is brought out for it, but no sooner does the poor thing approach water than fears are entertained in case it should be drowned. I wonder what it lives on? It has a most unpleasant odour, and we often wish it could escape and be seen and smelled no more by any of us.

I have once more tuned my guitar and made resolutions about practising it regularly, but all our spare time is at present devoted to our gardens, which quite repay the trouble we take with them. We are rejoicing also over many lovely wild flowers. At Christmas the gay blandfordia grandiflora is in its full glory, and the lovely fringed violet, which is a marked contrast, is also very plentiful.

On 23rd December my uncle returned from Sydney, accompanied by the Honble Captain Hope, a brother of the Earl of Hopeton, and certainly the tallest man I have ever met. On Christmas day most of the party went on the lake for a

AT LAKE INNES (1843)

sail. I stayed at home to fill the epergne, but first had to go to the lower lawn to be initiated into the art of catching grasshoppers, which is a very laborious undertaking. I would go as many months without fish rather than undertake to catch half-a-dozen grasshoppers. Mr Massie and Mr Montgomerie dined, in addition to our house party. It was very late when dinner was announced, the cook imagining it was a holiday (and making it one) had gone to sleep.

Chapter

6

PERIL IN THE SURF
1844

O<small>N NEW YEAR'S DAY</small> we were all up very early, having arranged to walk to the sandy flat off the beach road to get native flowers. Mr Hugh Mackay went with us and Margaret —only fancy Margaret! She tried to escape, but could not. Mrs Haloran, of course, hastened to open the gate and wish us many happy new years, adding, "Ye'll have a fine bogie (bathe) this morning." So we told Mr Hugh he had been promoted, as he was now a Companion of the Bath! We got a great many fine blandfordias and some ipomœas, and got home in time to arrange flowers for the library and decorate the breakfast table. In the afternoon I arranged the flowers for the epergne. They really were splendid, but alas! before they reached the dining-room the airy fabric was upset. The tallest blandfordias which supported a long wreath of passion flowers was raised so high that they touched the top of the door and went over at once— rather a trial to my temper at the moment.

Mrs M'Leod, Miss Marion, and Hector arrived at four o'clock to dine and stayed all night. Mr Alec Macleod, Mr Gray and Capt. Hunter were in time for dinner. We were a party of sixteen. Afterwards we danced, first on the lawn and then in what was the pink room, but is now our dancing and recreation room. I danced the Haymakers with Gustavus, but had some fear of losing him among so many grown-up people.

2nd January. I was not dressed in time to see Mrs M'Leod before she left, which was at six o'clock. I raced down to the gate but was just too late. Got some granadillas and gathered leaves for my "beastie", and Captain Hope brought me a fresh branch of gum-tree for it. It is an immense red caterpillar, with some purple and some black spots on it. It has a hard tail, which it strikes against the side of its box if you touch it. It is a sphinx. Captain Hope found it and brought it in. I cannot say that I have much regard for the creature, but I mean to keep it and see what it will turn into.

The gentlemen all left about two o'clock. It seems quite an age since we have been alone. I believe the first action of each and all of us was to take a good sound sleep. Then we went to the garden and got a liberal supply of grapes.

5th January. Everything has been taken out of the drawing-room and the floor taken up, as the joists which support it were giving way. They have been attacked by white ants, and I wonder they did not give way long ago, for, on opening a chiffonier which stands in the room, the lower part was found to be quite filled with earth and these destructive little creatures. They had made their way through the floor and through the bottom of the chiffonier. Dwarf walls of brick are to be built to support the new joists, and these are to be coated with tar. The earth deposited in the chiffonier was quite hard, but pierced by many narrow tunnels, and embedded in it was a set of beautifully carved ivory chessmen, which, with some other things, had been put carefully away. With time and trouble the chessmen were restored, but nothing else.

Sunday 7th January. Went to church, but the heat was so great we drove, as Gordy said, "tremendously slowly". Dido did not feel well, so I went with her to The Stores, where the horses are always put up. We were shewn into a nice cool room. Mrs Gloag received us very kindly, and was most pleasant, and I think glad to see us. She does not seem to know anyone in Port Macquarie. Mr Gloag showed us rather a curious ornament, which at first I thought was china. He said he kept it in remembrance of a favourite horse which was drowned at the wharf. The ornament was made from the shoulder bone of the horse, and is painted to look like a clergyman in his gown. It is very well done, and has a very good effect. I have often seen bones of the same shape lying about and called "the Parson" but had no idea why, and that it was so good an outline of one.

9th January. Got up very early and walked to the beach, where we had a delightful bathe, but came back starving and exhausted, as we had forgotten to take anything with us to eat. We meant to spend a very quiet evening, but Dr Stacy, Mr Solway, and Mr Graham arrived. My uncle had returned the day before. Mr Graham is most indignant with Mr ———, whom we think so clever and well informed. It seems that when he leaves home he locks his door (an unpardonable offence, and not at all usual in the bush). He had also been known to seal up the

*"We got up early
and walked to the beach."*

PERIL IN THE SURF (1844)

key, so that no traveller may be admitted during his absence, and there is no food to be had, unless you take some of the servants' rations, which, of course, is out of the question. Lately Mr G. and Mr R. were travelling in that direction, and finding the hospitable owner of the station was from home, and the door of his house locked, they attacked a passion-vine which he had trained with great care, so as to give the fruit the full benefit of the sunshine, and, in my opinion, behaved very greedily by eating it all.

Friday, 19th January. There was a violent thunderstorm. My uncle, coming back from the settlement, got quite wet through. Capt Hope, who had walked to Tacking Point, also got a benefit. He brought back with him some beautiful white flowers which we discovered in the vases after dinner, and I immediately came upstairs to sketch one, as they fade very rapidly.

27th January. We have had some miserably wet days, and only one walk to the beach, where we had a delightful bathe. When we were dressing we thought we saw some people coming towards us and were in much excitement, when, to our surprise, they proved to be three large native dogs. One had a large fish in his mouth; all were very bold, and came quite near us.

Our schoolroom work progresses. We have begun mathematics, but my present knowledge extends little beyond the fact that "a line is length without breadth." We, however, proved the first question with my aunt's aid. She has more patience than any one I know. We are now having Cowper's "Praise of the Country", which is difficult after the school pieces we have had lately. I generally have some confidence in my memory, and will now have an opportunity of trying it.

Lately we met Mr Murrigat again (a black fellow) but he did not show much anxiety to renew our acquaintance, though he explained to me how his wife, Ellen, "when she was a little boy" had had the first joint of her little finger cut off to enable her to roll up her fishing tackle with more ease.

The home mail is in, and mamma has had a letter from her

Aunt Louisa, an old maid who lives in Devonshire. I narrowly escaped having to answer it at once. I have been asking about some of my ancestors, and find that Grandpapa Campbell's mother was a Miss Fogo, aunt to Sir John Moore, who, therefore, was his first cousin, first and second to my mother, and first and third to me. Well, I would be proud had he been my twenty-third, but even Scotchmen, I am told, do not count kin beyond the sixteenth generation.

Jam-making has been the order of the day. I had some mending to do—oh! hateful task—but could not resist joining the party in the garden, who were gathering grapes. Afterwards we were very merry picking them off the branches and weighing them and the sugar preparatory to the boiling which Christina and Helen undertook, and mamma superintended.

29th January. When we sat down to breakfast this morning Captain Hope was not to be found. Someone suggested Tacking Point as the attraction, and sure enough about ten o'clock he returned, bringing a large bunch of beautifully fresh white orchids, one of which I began at once to paint. My aunt had shewn him my first attempt, and all he said was: "It may be well drawn, but no one would recognize in it the flower that grows at Tacking Point." So naturally I was disappointed, and anxious to do better, especially as he had so kindly brought us these lovely fresh flowers. Happily, the result was satisfactory to all, and the critic pronounced that it would do very well.

The steamer could not get out owing to the state of the bar or the tide, or both, so the gentlemen who were going to Sydney came back, and we had a very merry evening, ending with a Christmas game called flour pudding, for which Captain Hope was answerable. My experience of it is that once a year is once too often. A basin of flour was brought into the dining-room and turned out on a large dish, and sixpence placed on the top. Each person then cuts a slice in turn; the unfortunate who cuts down the sixpence has then to have the pleasure of rubbing it off the dish with his nose. At first all were most careful, then someone jogged his neighbour's elbow—down came the sixpence. Some flour was thrown in return, and it ended in a grand game of romps for a few minutes, each trying to shew the effect of powder on their neighbour's head. Captain Hope fared the best; he is so tall. Then a glass of water was upset; the floor became a slide, and we flew from the room.

Tuesday, 6th February 1844. I have been thus particular in recording the date, as this was one of the most eventful days of my life, so far at least as being in great danger of losing it goes. The weather had been wet and stormy for some days, but as it had cleared we set off about four o'clock for a walk to the beach, taking our bathing dresses with us, as we hoped we might be able to bathe. The roads were very wet and we did not keep very well together, so when we arrived at the beach Christina and the children were already in the water, but keeping well to the edge of the waves as the sea was dreadfully rough. Dido and I got ready, though we thought we ought to wait for my mother, but seeing her on the bank we quieted our consciences and raced down to the water and were soon over heads and ears dashing about. We next began to explore our bathing place, for the whole beach had been very much changed by the late storm. Our bathing place is usually a gradual sandy slope towards the sea, but today it was gravelly with a steep descent of about two feet, and further out a sand bank, which when the tide receded was left almost dry, thus leaving a narrow channel, the water in which was in continual agitation from the waves dashing in at each end and meeting.

Dido had scrambled off to some rocks in the direction of Cati Creek. I do not know what tempted me to follow, but it was fortunate I went, for no sooner had I caught her hand than a great wave lifted her completely off her feet, and I had great difficulty in balancing myself on a rock upon which only one foot was resting, while the water washed about with what appeared to me unusual force. How thankful I was for being tall: it was the first time I had ever found the advantage of it. Dido was completely out of her depth and quite powerless.

Fortunately she did not attempt to move. I held her by the shoulder and had just sufficient strength to keep her head above water. We were about a minute in that frightful position, and I scarcely know how we got on shore. We spoke not a word, and scarcely looked at each other till we were far up on the dry sand, and then Dido said she had never been so frightened or felt so near death as the moment before, the feeling of having nothing to rest her feet on was so dreadful. I agreed that we had no doubt been in great danger, and for a moment we were very serious, then our fears vanished, and we were dipping in the water as madly as ever.

I cannot think what possessed us, or where my small portion of commonsense had flown to; it really was a tempting of Providence, but my mother joined us and we felt reassured again. She was showing us how to swim, for the tide was coming in, and the water in the little channel was now pretty deep. Suddenly Margaret exclaimed, "There is a large wave coming!" I scrambled in as fast as I could, but it overtook me. On recovering from the shock I looked round for the others, and saw mamma beside me. I closed my eyes again and heard her exclaim, "Dido! Annabella!" I looked up. Oh! who can describe the horror, the agony of that moment? Dido was floating some yards from us quite helplessly, being borne out to sea by the force of the receding wave. An indescribable feeling of horror crept over me —I felt as if it depended on me to save her.

I started forward, but she was out of my sight. In a moment she rose again; her face was turned towards us, her arms stretched out. The sight gave me fresh courage; another plunge, and I, too, was quite out of my depth, and as completely at the mercy of the waves as my cousin. I stumbled on some sharp rocks; the pain was unheeded. My only distinct remembrance is on rising again finding myself almost within arm's length of her. I bent forward, but she sank, and in a second rose at least a yard further out. Oh! that fearful moment; it makes me shudder now when I think of it. I felt perfectly sick— sank again, and almost gave up all hopes of reaching her.

"Oyster Bay, Port Macquarie 1841" — *Henry Curzon Allport*
(Hastings River Historical Society)

PERIL IN THE SURF (1844)

106

Mamma was struggling on beside me, sinking and rising, and equally determined with myself not to return without Dido.

But what must Margaret's feelings have been; she it was who first warned us of the danger, and now stood almost petrified. She saw Dido swept off by the wave, and mamma and me rush after her, saw us all rising and sinking, not knowing which of us might first be washed for ever from her sight. She describes it as the most frightful nightmare. She tried to scream, tried to move forward, but was unable. When she came to herself again she was still standing in the same spot with her hands tight clasped, but we? We were safe on the beach. A wave had washed Dido towards us. I had caught her outstretched hand, and extending the other to my mother we had together been washed on shore. The moment I felt we were in safety my full tide of animal spirits returned, and I felt—I cannot say how I felt. I could neither laugh or cry, but I was very happy and thankful. My dear mother was quite overcome. She knelt upon the sand and thanked the Most High for our happy deliverance; she looked so pale and ill that I was beginning to feel very much alarmed about her. Then she rose and called Dido to her.

Margaret, in her joy, was dragging her as far from the sea as she could. We were all now assembled, an odd-looking group in our wet bathing dresses, and our long hair streaming round us. Mamma sat on the sand very pale and her lips perfectly blue. Dido was just recovering her recollection, for though she showed wonderful presence of mind while in the water, she says that just as someone caught her hand she had given up all hope of being saved, the pain of the water coming in at her ears, nose and mouth being quite stupefying. It must have been a terrible feeling. Margaret stood, her hand pressed to her forehead, while Gordy and Tay were pictures of horror and surprise. Christina joined us at that moment. She had not observed us till we had reached the shore, and her first idea was that we had been attacked by a shark, as we were so dreadfully cut and bruised.

She said, "Deed, I didna know what to think when I saw you, I didna know whether to laugh or to cry, for I thought a shark had bit my mistress, so I counted her feet, and then Miss Annabella gave me such a queer look I burst out laughing;" and so it was Christy's laugh that broke the spell. We then all hurried off to dress, and to leave the beach.

I took one parting look at the sea. The water seemed to boil over the very spot we had been bathing in, which by its formation allowed the waves to rush in on three sides, and sometimes they met with a tremendous crash: it really was quite frightful. We held a consultation as to where, when, and how, our adventure should be related, but we met my uncle and aunt before we reached the bridge, so the whole story was told at once to our infinite satisfaction. It was a most delightfully calm evening when I came upstairs, and I could not help throwing up the window and looking out. The moon was under a cloud, but the stars shone brightly, while the sea was roaring dreadfully. How nearly we were being left in it this evening, and what deep cause of thankfulness we have that we were not drowned. Assuredly we had no part in saving ourselves. Had Dido not been thrown towards us when she was, she must have sunk, and we would have followed. No doubt we would have been thrown back on the beach, as the tide was coming in with great force. But where and how?—who can tell? I cannot bear to think of it.

I wish I could imitate Cardinal Chign, who, it is said, wrote for fifty years with one pen. I do not think he could have used it much, for mine requires to be mended very often, and I cannot always get a pen-knife. Much to our surprise, the ponies have at last been brought in, and Dido and Margaret have had some delightful rides. I have been spending a week with Mrs M'Leod in Port M'Quarie, where I remained after church on Sunday. In the afternoon we took a long walk, as there was no second service. After tea Mrs M'Leod read prayers and then a sermon.

PERIL IN THE SURF (1844)

On Monday Mr Hugh took me for a ride round Tacking Point. He had a very restless young horse, and I had Cupid, a spirited pony, which my uncle has lent to the boys. The road was quite charming, part of the way being through a scrub of lofty-leaved evergreens, festooned with graceful runners. A pathway had been cleared, but was rapidly growing up again. At the top of the hill a magnificent sea view broke on me quite unexpectedly; then we went down to the level sands, and no sooner had Cupid passed the little creek than he set off at full speed towards the rock. I did not attempt to stop him, and enjoyed the gallop very much, but was surprised at his readiness to stop and turn as soon as we reached the rocks till I heard it was a sort of training ground, and he had been accustomed to gallop there. I think they should have told me.

One day we rode to Thrumster, which is rather a pretty place. It belongs to my uncle, and is called after his father's place in Caithness. The house is too near the road to New England, but there is a good garden. It is about seven miles from Port

*"I have been spending
a week with Mrs M'Leod."*

M'Quarie, and the same distance from The Lake. Mr and Mrs Taylor, now of Terrible Valley, New England, used to live at Thrumster, and when they left there was an idea that we should settle there, but I am glad to say it was not carried out. We rode out by the long bridge and passed a large dry swamp, which, I believe, is some day to be converted into a racecourse.

Next day we rode to Blackman's Point, but had to return at once, as all the gentlemen were engaged to play cricket. There is a great extent of water, where the Wilson and Hastings Rivers meet, and Gooloowa, Captain Jobling's cottage, looked very pretty across the water. Coming back we admired the evergreens on each side of the road: they really are beautiful. The principal flower is the purple ipomœa, which is convolvulus and of a lovely colour. The vine grows most freely from tree to tree, its glossy leaves waving in rich masses covered with flowers. There were also quantities of myrtleberries, which grow in clusters, the branches bending under their weight. One day we made a variety of calls. Mrs Ackroyd is still a great invalid, and Marion kindly goes every day to read to her. The Ditmas family have at last started for New England: they have been going for the last six months. We were invited to tea by Mrs Richardson, but did not go till quite dark. We found a large party already assembled, and we were seven. Tea was handed round in the drawing-room by an old man, who handed also muffins and biscuits, but he seemed to think that because I did not take two cups of tea I could not eat two pieces of bread and butter.

After tea we looked at some prints, and talked or were silent till it was proposed that we should dance, so we adjourned to another room which was not very spacious, and Mr Gorman played the flute while we danced a set of quadrilles. Then Miss Fatherini was pressed to sing, but drew back with apparent unwillingness till they ceased to ask her. Then she supposed she must sing, and finally began "She Wore a Wreath of Roses". We danced again, and ended up with a game called "The Rusty Rapier". Trays were brought in with sandwiches,

110

etc., before we left. We had a pleasant walk home, though the
air was keen and cold, and the night pitch dark.

Next day we rode again to Tacking Point, taking the beach
road, which is quite beautiful, but the path in some parts was
dangerously steep and narrow. We were a large party, and
enjoyed a good gallop on the sands. At four o'clock we went
to the Manse, where Mr Purvis read the sixth chapter of
"Watts on the Mine" and part of the first book of Milton's
Paradise Lost, which he explained, and afterwards questioned
the members of his class. He also read some selections on
Memory and Testimony. I am sorry I shall not have an opportunity of attending another of these interesting readings.

On Saturday morning, about eight o'clock, I had the satisfac
tion of seeing the steamer pass my window. Miss M'Leod
arrived by it, and others of the wedding party are expected
next week. This house is two-storied, and joins the hotel, which
occupies the corner of the chief street near the landing pier.
There is only a wide road between the veranda and the sea.
I admired the view very much one morning as we watched
a boat loaded with grass coming from the opposite shore—
it was drawn into the current, and then carried rapidly down
past the house. The men stopped, and landed the grass. It was a
Government boat, and there were men in waiting, who soon
carried off its contents.

In the afternoon it was proposed that we should call at
Gooloowa, which I was glad to have an opportunity of doing.
Mr Hugh escorted us, and instead of going by the old long
bridge, we crossed the new one, which is scarcely finished—it
forms a dam also, and will be a fine wide roadway, very
different from the old one; there is a flood-gate in progress.
Arrived at Blackman's Point, we signalled for a boat, which
soon arrived to "row us o'er the ferry". It was manned by an
extraordinary-looking black boy, very short and badly made. He
had one long finger, which clasped the oar, while the others
were comparatively useless. This Point is formed by the junction
of the Hastings and Wilson Rivers. The Marie joins the

Hastings higher up. We were some time crossing, and together they form a fine sheet of water, very clear, but quite salt, and the tide comes up beyond Gooloowa. We walked up a sloping green bank to the cottage, which is situated in a pretty flower garden. There is a little island near the house, and another covered with mangroves further up. These, with the wide river and the distant hills, made a very pretty picture. We walked in the garden, then had some cake and wine, and the Misses Jobling shewed us some of their pretty work—imitation Brussels lace, and very fine open-worked knitted stockings and edgings. They have a good collection of butterflies, really worth having, and were delighted with the curious creature Mr Hugh M'Leod took over to them. It is green, and has a fat body, long anthers, and six legs, each like two small cactus leaves, quite as prickly, and exactly the colour. It certainly is the largest insect I have ever seen. The horses during our absence were tied up in a little yard at the side of the water. I was glad to find myself mounted again, as I seem not at all fond of being on the water.

Mr Gray and Mr Hay came in to spend the evening. The latter lost his way yesterday returning from Rolands Plains,[1] and had to spend the night in the bush. He had neither a light nor provisions, and his adventure was not an enviable one. He says he put his great-coat over his horse. It reminded me of a picture I have seen in a comic annual of an old woman standing in heavy rain while she sheltered her ducklings under her umbrella. I was quite sorry to say goodbye to my kind friends. Mrs M'Leod's industry is untiring. During that week she knitted three pairs of gloves for her sons, a tiny pair and a pair of long socks for baby Marsh, to be worn when travelling, for, of course, she is coming to the marriage; besides this, she worked a square in mamma's friendship cushion, and a corner for Hector to ground. Marion was busy finishing a patchwork table cover of silk, the pieces cut in diamond shape of three different shades. These, when sewn together, form rows like

[1] Now Rolland's Plains.

boxes. The effect is very good. She kindly gave me the patterns, and we at once looked out all our pieces of silk and began to make one for my aunt.

18th July. My uncle, Mr Taylor, and Mr James Mackay left for Yarrow, and two Messrs M'Leod were to join them. Lachye would think they meant to take the place by storm. We took a long walk, and visited the myrtleberries, which are now in full bearing and quite beautiful. We picked some Cape-goose-berries. The plants are now spreading so rapidly that people begin to say they must be indigenous.

Sunday, 28th July, was Margaret's fifteenth birthday. We celebrated it by a great cake-making, a feast and games at "Les Graces", it being too wet to go out. Gustavus presented her with a string of small shells and two bead rings, all threaded by himself. My cuffs were finished in good time, and much admired.

The weather during the whole of July was very cold. I find by my journal that the 22nd was the coldest night of the season. Next day we were going to ride, and I went to the garden to cut a spruce stick to serve as a riding whip, but rain came on, and continued with little intermission for more than ten days. One day we ventured as far as the beach. The road was in a dreadful state, and at the poultry yard there was quite a little lake, in which the geese were swimming with evident enjoyment. Coming home there was a shower and a beautiful rainbow over the sea. Next day the rain fell in torrents all day, and during the night the wind rose and burst open one of the windows on the look-out, and I was awakened by the rain dropping on to the schoolroom floor. The following day was one of the calmest and brightest I ever remember, but, of course, we could not go to church. We hear of floods everywhere, rivers impassable, and bridges under water.

Thursday, 8th August. Had a delightful ride yesterday, and Dido and I have been busy today drawing the flowers and berries we brought home. Mr Purvis called and told us Miss Marion M'Leod has had a very bad fall from her horse. Her face is much cut and bruised, which just now is particularly unfortunate. I have been very busy in my garden, but the mischievous puppies have scratched up all the seeds. I cannot have even the poor satisfaction of beating them, for in the first place I cannot catch them, and in the second because my cousins would highly disapprove.

14th August. Our mania for gardening is over, and we have returned to "Les Graces" with double vigour. We have each got a new hoop, which we have covered according to our own taste and means. I kept up 379 with my aunt. We were surprised to hear that Lady, the bloodhound, had returned. It is curious how she found her way back, as she was taken by boat up the Marie, and could not know anything of the road. Her ungrateful puppy, Hector, did not recognize her.

On the morning of Saturday, 17th August, we received invitations from Mrs M'Leod for Tuesday, 20th, to Miss Marion's marriage. This we expected, but great was our surprise to hear there was to be a double marriage—Agnes Paterson to Mr Norman M'Leod—and that the bride and her father had just arrived by the steamer, and wished Margaret and me to be her bridesmaids—an office which we, of course, willingly accepted, our greatest difficulty being that our straw bonnets were newly trimmed with straw-coloured ribbon, and there was no white to be got. Some of the dresses in preparation were not yet finished, but Mrs Bruce took up her old place in the nursery with Christy and Jane, and, with mamma's able help and supervision, all were ready in good time. Of course we young people were equally busy. The household on Monday was astir by four o'clock. I finished the pincushion I was making for Miss Marion, and marked her initials and the date with pins. Margaret made a kettle-holder for her, and kindly gave up to me the cuffs I had worked for her birthday present, that I might give them to Agnes, and she gave her the collar to match. Then, as I was to be first bridesmaid, I thought it necessary to sew some lace on to my handkerchief. Gustavus had a new velvet jacket for his kilts. When everything was collected we were amused at the display of white dresses, no less than eight to be sent off in the cart, with neck ribbons, bows, berthes, etc., and a great variety of shoes: in short, two large trunks full. We could not drive to Port M'Quarie in our bridesmaids' dresses, and had to change again for the dance in the evening.

On Tuesday, 20th August—the eventful day—we set off for Port M'Quarie about nine o'clock. The roads were not so bad as we expected, but we had to turn off at the sandy flat, as the bridge was still under water. The morning was sufficiently cloudy to make us anxious about the weather, but was otherwise pleasant. The long bridge was in such a dilapidated condition it was thought it would not be prudent for us to cross it in the carriage. However, on arriving there, we found Bruce and two other men waiting for us, who, for greater security, walked by the horses' heads, and we soon found ourselves in safety at the other side. The servants, who had preceded us in the cart, had all things in readiness at The Stores, and assisted us to dress. We then drove to Mrs M'Leod's house.

The brides had not yet appeared, but the bridegrooms shone forth in all the splendour of white inexpressibles, and new coats, not to mention black beaver hats and white kid gloves. Miss M'Leod and I drove to the church with the brides. Mrs Marsh accompanied my aunt, as also Margaret, and my cousin. My uncle drove, and Mr M'Lean sat beside him. Mrs Paterson went in Mr Grey's gig, and all the rest of the party walked. Arrived at the steps leading up to the church, there was a great arranging as to how we were all to proceed. Mr Hugh M'Leod took Miss Marion, he being her especial brother. Mr Paterson had apparently forgotten his part and had to be called forward to offer his arm to his daughter, and the procession moved on up several short flights of steps to the church door, where we were met by Col. Grey, Miss Grey, and the Misses Jobling, who were also Marion's bridesmaids. Mr Cross had not yet put on his gown when we reached the altar, and when he did appear had to rest to recover his breath. However, he got through the ceremony better than was expected. It sadly failed in the solemnity it should inspire. I could scarcely help smiling at his precision about the ring, "Now, sir, the ring, put it on the book—on the book, sir. Now, sir, take it off the book, and put it on the fourth finger of your wife's left hand, put it over the knuckles, and hold it there and say after me 'With this ring', etc.," the same to both the bridegrooms. Unfortunately both the rings were rather small, and there was some difficulty in putting them over the knuckles. After the usual congratulations they went into my uncle's pew to sign the register. Mr M'Lean signed first, and the clerk, who did not seem to be very *au fait* at his duties, desired Agnes to sign hers under it, which would have been an awkward mistake.

Mrs Paterson's baby was christened before we left the church (Magnus Lloyd) Mr and Mrs Mordaunt M'Lean, and Mr Salway being sponsors. There were thirty of the marriage party, including little Aleck Paterson and Gustavus, who both appeared in Highland dress. There were a great many people looking on in church, and a crowd of children and servants. The newly married people went home in the carriage we came to church in. Some of the ladies accompanied my aunt. I was honoured with a place in his worship's gig, and everyone else walked. Now I must describe the dresses worn on the occasion. Marion's was of worked Indian muslin over a satin slip, a large white satin cardinal or demi-cloak, trimmed with swan's down, which I thought looked rather heavy. Agnes wore a white figured chalis, trimmed with gimp, and tassels at the sleeves, a small pointed cape of the same material setting off her pretty figure. Both brides wore white drawn silk bonnets with a fall of lace or veil sewed round, and both looked very well. The bruises on Marion's face had happily quite disappeared, and she looked very pretty, but older than her husband, which she is by more than a year. He is not yet twenty-one, and notwithstanding his sedulously cultivated whiskers looks very boyish. Marion had

four bridesmaids, her sister, Miss Grey, and the Misses Jobling.
They all wore white, with watered silk scarves and neck knots,
on each of which the bride had worked a tiny spray. Margaret
and I wore white checked muslin, with lace cardinals lined
with french white, and straw bonnets trimmed with the before-
mentioned straw-coloured ribbon.

We had cake and wine immediately on our return from the
church. The cake was large and uncommon looking—a small
cake on a large one. They made Agnes take off her ring, and
I passed a great many pieces of the cake through it for the
benefit of those unmarried friends who wished to dream on it.
In due time we were marshalled into lunch. There were two
tables, and I, being a first bridesmaid, was placed between Mr
Norman M'Leod and Capt. M'Lean. There were little bouquets
of flowers tied with white ribbon on each plate. The cake was
raised in the centre of the table, supported by an array of smaller
ones. The table was literally covered. I do not think it would
have held another glass, for in every crevice were placed
custards, jellies, and creams. At one end was the largest turkey
I ever saw, well supported by hams, tongues, chickens, ducks,
pies, tarts, puddings, blanc mange, and various fruits. In fact,

> The table groaned with costly piles of food,
> And all was more than hospitably good.

The ladies withdrew, and were soon joined by the gentlemen
after they had done due honour to the newly married pairs by
drinking their health with three cheers, and they had returned
thanks after the most approved style.

Now came the question as to how the afternoon could be
most agreeably wasted. It was with no little satisfaction we
heard there were carriages and gigs for all. The wind was
high, the roads muddy, and we did not wish to spoil our white
dresses. The bridegrooms each seized a gig and whisked off
their brides so rapidly that they were out of sight before we
were packed into our carriages. Fortunately, there was a good
proportion of very little people—Miss Grey, the Misses Jobling,

Dido, and Margaret inside, while Gordy and I sat on the box with Mr Magnus M'Leod driving, and six gentlemen outriders. We took the Tacking Point road, and had not gone very far when we stuck in the mud, and two traces were broken. Fortunately, Roderick, who had got another gig, overtook us. Into this gig we had all to step by turns and drive a few yards, the ground about the carriage being so muddy. After all, Mr Magnus and Mr Hugh had to pull it out, while Hector rode back for fresh traces. Roderick drove off in triumph, taking Miss Annie Jobling and Margaret, while we five distressed damsels looked enviously after them, and were left to make our way as best we could along the muddy road, though I own I saw no advantage to be gained by walking at all, especially as my shoes were very thin and rather tight. At length the carriage reappeared, and Mr Gray helped us in again. Our escort remounted their impatient steeds; smack went the whip, whirl went the wheels, and we returned to the town in great style, passing the other carriage in which my aunt and mamma had been making some calls. What is a drive without an adventure, especially on such an occasion?

Meantime, for our greater convenience, our trunks had been taken to Mrs M'Leod's, and we were shown into a room to change our dresses, where our chief anxiety was disinterested attempts to get each other dressed and out of the way, in which I was so supremely successful I was just down in time to get a cup of coffee before dancing began. The veranda was completely covered in with flags and sails, and lighted by lamps: it looked very well.

We began to dance about eight o'clock. The brides and bridegrooms opened the ball. They should have danced a minuet or some such old-fashioned piece of elegance to complete their return to the almost obsolete custom of remaining to join in the wedding festivities. The brides, of course, wore their wedding dresses, with pretty lace berthes, and looked very well. Agnes and Miss Stephen were the rival belles. The first has the best figure, but Miss Stephen has a profusion of beautiful fair hair, and is very graceful—certainly a great contrast to her brother, who is short and dark.

I must, of course, say something of the dresses worn on the occasion. Mrs Richardson appeared in black satin, made also too fashionably for our uneducated tastes. It looked as if she had a row of tiny aprons pendent from her waist, or an assortment of large reticules, while a small flower garden flourished in her hair. Mrs Purvis and Mrs Gorman wore light coloured satins. Mrs March, a figured white satin, her wedding dress I suppose. Mrs Danvers, all in black, looked ghastly; another lady wore a pretty light blue silk, on which there was a sad want of trimming. Her appearance reminded me of the Irish lady's question when invited to dine at —— house—"Do they strip their necks for dinner?" Hers was extra well done, and there was neither lace nor ornament to relieve the eye. Miss Fatherini's dress was high necked and long sleeved, her hair, as usual raised on a wall of plaits above her forehead, in imitation of a laurel wreath. You will think there was a scarcity of young gentlemen when I say that Capt. M'Lean was my best partner, but I have rather a penchant for old gentlemen, and may add that with his light brown wig and nimble dancing, no one would have supposed he was celebrating his son's marriage. After supper I played a set of quadrilles and some waltzes. I must not forget to say that as soon as we returned from church Miss M'Leod put on green stockings. I do not know the origin of the custom that when a younger sister marries the elder wears green stockings! Mr Solway's dress in the evening was unexceptionable, but I am told that in the morning Mr Cross asked him if he really meant to be God Father in the coat he had on.

Wednesday, 21st August. Slept most profoundly, and awoke at last to the recollection that the day we had been looking forward to for so long was now over. We certainly had enjoyed it, and would remember it with pleasure, but my head ached, and my feet were swollen. I could not get on my dancing

120

shoes, and the others had been sent away together with our
dark dresses, so we had to put on the white ones. Fortunately
it was a good day. All was in confusion packing and tidying,
so we said goodbyes to those who were leaving by the steamer,
and went to see Mrs Gorman. Her sister had already left
for the morning on horseback with her brother, and expected
to sleep that night in the bush. We then went to The Stores, as
my uncle wished to see mamma. We found him in his office,
and had a peep at the celebrated glass house. I had no time
to notice anything but the great size of the building. It seemed
greatly out of proportion with the rest of the town, as does
also the Royal Hotel, which is a handsome brick building.
Called on Mrs Richardson, who seemed to be holding a levée,
then by appointment to meet the carriage at Mrs M'Leod's,
but finding the broken traces were still unmended, we remained
to lunch, making a party of thirteen, which is said to be
unlucky, at least in so far as that the same thirteen will never
sit down together again. In this present instance this more
than probable. Colonel and Miss Grey came out to the Lake
for a few days, her first visit. She sings very sweetly, and we
all liked her very much.

On Saturday, 25th, a quantity of loquats were preserved, and
we helped to pick and prepare the fruit. After lunch my uncle
took us out on the lake, and allowed us to row ourselves,
which we enjoyed immensely. The water was like glass, and
reminded us forcibly of the lines in Parnell's "Hermit",
beginning—

> Thus when a smooth expanse receives impressed
> Calm Nature's image on her watery breast,
> Down bend the banks, the trees depending grow,
> And skies beneath with answering colours glow.

As we divided the water with our oars we watched them all
"in thick disorder run". We saw a large flock of wild ducks
which allowed us to come quite near them.

Monday, 26th August. Resumed our usual occupations with renewed pleasure, and declared it as quite a holiday to have lessons again. However, on Wednesday we were quite happy to receive Mrs M'Leod and a party of eight, who arrived soon after lunch to spend the day and dine. Others arrived later, so we were a party of sixteen, and seven in the schoolroom, where the three young gentlemen were delighted to take tea. I called on them on my way down to dinner and was much amused at the way in which the boys started up exclaiming fourth, fifth, sixth. After some explanation I found they wanted to engage me for the fourth, fifth, and sixth dances, and as this was to be their last evening here, I gave the required promise. When the dancing began this gave great offence to the elders of the party, and Mr Hay made a formal complaint of me to myself! At dinner I sat opposite Mr Alister M'Lean, and when the epergne was removed felt much inclined to say "how do you do" to him. It was a gorgeous erection of flowers. I was thankful to see it carried off without accident, as it was that in which I was most concerned.

On Friday, Hector and Harold came to lunch, and to say a last farewell. They are going to Sydney, and Mrs M'Leod intends soon to go on a round of visits to her sons and married daughters.

Wednesday, 4th September. Played "Les Graces" with Mr Graham before breakfast, and he kept up 1500, when the bells sounded and we had to stop. We have since then had some very pleasant rides, and been several times on the Lake.

On the 6th Mr Gray called and he told us that the post boy who every one supposed had been drowned, or robbed, or killed, or had run away, had only been detained by the Commissioners on account of the floods. We saw a wild pheasant on the gravel in front of the house, the first I have ever seen, it is rather a pretty bird, brown, with a long tail. Mr Hugh M'Leod has given Dido his pet cockatoo. It barks like a dog and makes the usual pretty speeches in its own praise, though Gustavus comes in triumphantly declaring that Cockey had said that he was a pretty boy.

7th September. The gentlemen left after breakfast to attend Dr Carlisle's funeral. He died on Thursday morning rather suddenly, and was buried today at Hamilton. A great many people were present, Mr Purvis officiating, as Mr Cross could not do so without permission from the Bishop. It is a strange desire, I think, wishing to be buried in a lawn or garden, when living within easy reach of a Churchyard. Mrs Dutton (Mrs Stephen's eldest daughter) is also buried at Hamilton. She was, I believe, a very beautiful girl, and was married at the early age of fourteen. She died when only seventeen—her tombstone bears the single word "Claudia"—hers was a brief sad life.

11th September. My uncle returned from Sydney, bringing with him Mr Sydney Darling, a nephew of Captain Dumaresq, and son of the Governor of that name. He is fond of boating, and my uncle has taken us out on the lake several times. One day the wind was very high and contrary, so we were thankful when at sundown we were landed in perfect safety. The gentlemen were very good in rowing, but we breathed a sigh of relief, when, next day they all rode off to Rollands Plain.

One evening Mr Darling put on his full uniform for our benefit; it is the handsomest I have seen, and the wearer looked handsome too, but so very tiny.

Lake Innes, 17th September 1844, Tuesday. Well, I really am quite eighteen now, and I have been wishing all day that yesterday had been my sixteenth birthday; so you see that already I have arrived at the age when ladies wish to be thought younger than they really are. My wishes are much more extensive than that, for I not only desire to be thought young, but to be so. There are also some new ideas gaining ground in my wise head, and, seriously speaking, I feel there is much room for improvement and correction, and I hope my endeavours may be strengthened, and that I may not only feel but act on those feelings.

We resumed our usual studies. I think we spend the mornings more agreeably than most people. About four o'clock the steamer was seen passing slowly south, tugging a small sailing vessel which is not yet completed. Enjoyed a walk by myself in the garden, which is looking beautiful with honeysuckle and other spring flowers, and the lovely Cape bulbs just coming into flower. The sandy flat near the beach is gay with many colours, this being the best month here for wild flowers.

20th September. Mrs M'Leod and Roderick arrived to spend a few days. She, of course, brought an ample supply of work. My uncle and Mr Fenwick arrived at dark from Yarrows, the latter as fond as ever of waltzing. I longed to present him with a pair of gloves.

On Sunday, 22nd, we went to church. The wind became so boisterous we could scarcely hear a word of the service. Between twelve and one o'clock it blew a hurricane; fortunately it subsided, and we got home safely.

On the 23rd Jane left for New England with her brother. She came to my room before daylight to say goodbye. We shall miss her, though she is so remarkably quiet, besides which we shall have some of her duties to perform, such as keeping the schoolroom in order. She is not strong, so her brothers, who are married, wish her to visit them. I have just finished painting a curious-looking green flower. It grows about eight inches from the ground, with only one flower on each stem—(*Pterostylus*). We have gathered lately a quantity of Cape-gooseberries and wild raspberries at the back of the hill. Mr Fenwick told us a story of Midger Brown, a black boy my uncle used to take about with him and whom he dressed very smartly and spoiled very much. One day at the club in Sydney, where there happened to be a good number of gentlemen staying, Midger began asking them for money. Some gave it to him, others promised to do so. Mr Fenwick did neither, upon which Midger asked indignantly why he had not given him half-a-crown. He replied that he could not afford it. Oh, then, said Midger, if you are a poor man and cannot afford to give half-a-crown, I will give you one, putting his hand into his pocket as he spoke. However, he did not take it out again —imagine the impertinence of this creature. We have been busy pasting some pictures into Mrs M'Leod's larger scrap-book, which she left with us; it is really a most interesting collection.

Monday, 30th September. Went to church yesterday. There has been a small gallery put up for the Seraphines, but I do not observe any difference in the music. I never saw so many people in church, and there was a great assemblage at the church door after service and much shaking of hands, as Mrs M'Leod's family are leaving to-day—a double hands-shaking, as goodbye was even more necessary than "how do you do". We had to walk across the bridge; it is now in such a dilapidated condition, and instead of finishing off the dam so that it can be used, it is being made wider.

There was an immense fire at the lake last night. It looked quite splendid. The natives had set the reeds on fire, and at one time it was feared that the boat house was in danger, so men were sent down to clear a space round it. We had strawberries and cream today; there is every prospect of a good crop this year. The bees which swarmed on my birthday have been most industrious. The honey looks beautiful, and the wax perfectly white. On Saturday morning when my aunt came to the school-room she said we were all to go to the drawing-room at once and wait for her, as she had something very particular for us to do. We, of course, were all anxiety to find out what it was, but did not feel any wiser when she reappeared bringing a saucer with whitening in it, some water, and several white cloths. Now what do you think we were going to do? To clean the windows! We set to work very busily, Margaret and Dido, Gordy, and I, but my partner was so little I had to get Mr Hugh Mackay to take her place, and though I say it that should

PERIL IN THE SURF (1844)

not, we were the most industrious of the party, and cleaned no less than seven French windows without breaking a single pane. My uncle came to see us, and nodded approval, and we all quite enjoyed ourselves. I have no idea why we were set to this work, or who usually did it.

After lunch we got ready to ride. I never saw such a wild creature as Mr Hugh's horse. After kicking and plunging it broke away, and set off at full gallop, and though Mr Patrick and one of the grooms went after it they could not catch it, and he had to take another. We rode to Tacking Point.

Murrigate has brought us another young swan, and a supply of reeds, which he cut up very scientifically for its use. This is the fourth we have had this season. Two died, and one got away when it was half grown, so we hope it got safely to the lake.

8th October. We finished learning the fifth book of Milton's *Paradise Lost*, and are all delighted with it, though we do not exactly "dance for joy". Our other poetry lesson just now is Goldsmith's *Deserted Village*, which is a very favourite piece of mine. Gathered Cape-gooseberries, and worked in my garden, which has some beautiful bulbs in flower, but I cannot persuade Sweet William to flourish in it, much to my regret. Some time ago I made an ornamental fence of peach sticks to divide it. Like Robinson Crusoe's hedge, they are all growing.

About this time my uncle made up his mind to have a vineyard of thirty acres planted, which was the extent thought desirable at that time to have in full bearing before starting seriously to the business of wine-making. The first thing to be done was to select the ground, and have it cleared and trenched. The spot chosen adjoined the fruit garden, and was bounded on the west by the road to Port M'Quarrie. The ground was covered with small trees and shrubs, and in it stood three gigantic bluegum-trees, the largest on the property, and I think the largest I have ever seen. It took weeks to dig them out by the roots. I see by my journal that the first fell with a tremendous crash on 8th October, and I regret very much that the measurements were not taken at the time. It took a long time to prepare the ground. I never saw it in full bearing, but I know it was planted with the choicest vines. After my uncle's death in 1857, his son, who was a great temperance advocate, would not have any wine made, and allowed the vineyard to become overgrown. Eventually it was, I believe, destroyed by a bush fire, and the wine-cellars went to ruin. There were other small vineyards started in the neighbourhood about the same time, but I do not know with what result.

15th October. The fifteenth anniversary of my uncle's and aunt's marriage. Of course we had a holiday and a pic-nic. We found luncheon laid out in state in our newly-discovered bower near the lake. It is formed by swamp-oak trees. On our way home we found a beautiful passion-vine growing luxuriantly over a fallen tree, and with a quantity of fruit on it.

Mr H. Mackay has made a stand for measuring horses marked in inches and half inches, and we have all been measured by it. I am 5ft 8¼in., but I am determined to drop the ¼in. I am sure it must be a mistake. Dido is equally sure that she is 5ft 2in., though that badly marked stand made her only 5ft 1in. After dinner we danced, but we had all been up so early and so busy all day, we were quite tired.

18th October. Dr and Mrs Richardson came to lunch and to spend the afternoon, bringing their eldest son and little girl. It was a farewell visit, as they all leave for Sydney next week. They will be very much missed. Dr Richardson is a very old friend of ours. He is a colonial surgeon, and was stationed at Bathurst in 1826. We walked in the garden; the weather is delightful. All nature seems clad in its gayest dress. The acacias are lovely, with their graceful drooping flowers. Honeysuckle, Jessamine, and all roses are in their prime, and the scent of orange, lemon, and shaddock blossom quite delightful. The Cape bulbs are still in great beauty. They are various in colour, and planted as they are in beds they look rather gaudy. The

PERIL IN THE SURF (1844)

creepers[1] that were planted at the new arches are growing fast, and those that were planted two years ago have quite filled in some of the arches, giving them the appearance of a wall where they have not been pruned or trained. The various passion-vines are coming into flower, and there are masses of other vines and creepers—maurandia, barclayana, cobia, etc.

21st October. It was oppressively hot all the morning, but at three o'clock a thunder shower cleared the air delightfully. I love the scent of the earth after rain.

> A fresher green the smelling leaves display,
> And, glittering as they tremble, cheer the day.

26th October. Mr Grey brought us the music and a paper with a description of the Porkie, the new dance he has been talking so much about. We now discover it to be the Polka. I have copied the music and am learning it, though we do not think it particularly pretty. It is a Polish dance, I believe, and, judging from the pictures of the dancers, one would require to see it danced and to be taught before attempting it. Walked to the poultry yard and visited the old man who now has charge of it instead of Mrs Haloran, who, poor woman, has been very ill and moved into one of the cottages at the back of the house. The man was a sailor in Nelson's own ship, and wounded at, I think, the battle of Trafalgar. I was amused at his way of speaking, and thought that the speeches one reads of as being made by sailors are not far wrong. Our old sailor used such long words. He invited us to inspect the coveys of chickens, and described the audaciousness of the native dogs, which thought nothing of coming patrolling up and down between his house and the pig-sties. Finally he accompanied us to the gate, and said he was quite out of baccy—also expressed his surprise that the mistress did not "consider to allow him proper drinking vessels for the fowls, for indeed, Miss, I have never nothing, nothing unless I take a broken bottle, or, Miss, the heel of my shoe."

[1] Now known as the Innes Curse.

Of course we kept Hallowe'en, but the fortunes predicted are so very different from last year that my faith has been rather shaken in them.

We have devoted the last few days to the study of the *Illustrated London News*. Dr Stacey kindly lent us a large parcel of them. One of the chief subjects in these numbers is her Majesty's progress through the different counties, with drawings of the splendid archway through which she passed. It is quite a Court paper, even the Queen's fowl-house is there, and drawings of her favourite pets.

2nd November. We heard from my aunt, Mrs Ranken, today. She has another son; he was born on the 19th of last month. We were much surprised to hear of the dreadful flood there has been on the Lauchlan. They were all obliged to hasten from the house at Glen Logan, leaving clothes, boots, and everything but a few blankets snatched hastily from the beds. They had then to walk ten miles to the nearest shelter, the rain pouring in torrents and the water often knee deep. Annabella M'Leod, who was staying with my aunt, wrote the letter, and had promised to send further particulars of the flood and their flight. We have great cause for thankfulness that they escaped without accident.

It is reported that some families lower down the river have been swept away. The accounts from the Hawkesbury and Argyll country are truly distressing. Near a place called Gundagi, a shepherd who had gone out in the morning with his flock, was unable to return home owing to the rise of the water which was rapidly surrounding the hut in which were his wife and four children. His anxiety about them was very great, for though he was within a short distance of the hut the rapid current prevented the possibility of his approaching it. The next morning he was thankful to find his family were all in safety in a tree into which they had been helped by a man who, fortunately, arrived at the hut intending to spend the night there. They remained in the tree four days till the water subsided, their only food being a fowl they caught by chance, and were obliged to eat raw.

Sunday morning we spent in the schoolroom, and wrote out from memory as far as we have learned of the 119th Psalm. It is by far the most difficult we have yet learned. The constant repetition of the same words, or words with the same meaning, make it most puzzling.

Monday, 4th. We all three rode to the beach. We went as far as Grant's Head. The outlet to the sea at Cati Creek is quite closed, and safe to ride on for the first time for two years. At Ten Miles Creek we went up the bank from the beach and rode to the furthest point from which we would see Camden Haven River, and to the north Tackling Point. Our beach seemed quite in a bay coming home. We met some natives near the bridge, who had just set the grass on fire, and the flames frightened our horses.

Thursday, 7th November 1844. Dear mamma's birthday! I had got a cord and tassel from Sydney, and finished the bag I worked for her while she was away. Dido painted a bunch of violets for her. Of course we had luncheon out of doors, and there were many suggestions as to where we should pic-nic, but it was too hot to go far. We had the usual pies and pastry, but an unusual addition in a basket of oysters, and a jug of beer. In the evening we all played casino.

This was my dear mother's thirty-ninth birthday, which then appeared to us to be quite old. Now after a period of more than sixty years, I know that she was almost young, and a very handsome woman, above the middle height, healthy, active, and handsome in face and figure, a graceful rider, and Bruce (who was a judge) openly proclaimed that she danced better than any of us. I still remember with admiration the calm dignity of her manner. She had laid aside her widow's cap and deep mourning, but she always wore black. I think it was the following year that one of the numerous visitors to the Lake wrote to her proposing for one of her daughters. There was no hesitation as to the reply, but she thought it right to show the letter to my uncle. "Bless me," he exclaimed, "you astonish me, I thought he was *your* admirer." She was deeply wounded and said reproachfully, "Have I ever given anyone reason to say such a thing of me?" while he hastily corrected himself—"Your friend, friend, I should have said." The writer of the letter little knew the annoyance he had given them both.

8th November. The furniture has all been taken out of the library, and we were set to work to make a new carpet for it; a desperate undertaking it was, but we were all so anxious to assist that we were quite in each other's way. I was surprised at getting a little box from Port Macquarie, favoured by the Rev. Mr Woodward, the newly-appointed clergyman, and opened it in doubt if it was for Dido or myself. It contained a crayon drawing, a bust of Lord Londonberry, from Charlotte Stewart, and a long letter giving me all the Parramatta news.

11th November. A dinner party in honour of Mr Friell, who has just come from India. He has brought a number of coolies with him, intending to settle in this country. He is introduced to my uncle by his brother, Dr James Innes, and Aunt Jane Alicia. We have all got new riding habits of brown merino. I think I liked our old blue camlet better. Dido has till now always worn brown holland, and we all wore Panama hats. Our Scotch caps, made from a pattern of Aunt Barbara's, are quite a success. They are made of black velvet, drawn into a band of tartan satin round the head, and at the crown a large flat button with a cord and tassel to match the tartan. Gordy and Gustavus do not ride yet. They spend much of their time adorning their new bower. Jane used always to go with them, but now they are supposed to be old enough to take care of themselves. One afternoon they gave us a dreadful fright. Mamma and I were alone in the garden when we heard the most piercing screams coming from their direction. I thought it was scarcely possible for them to make so much noise, but ran at once to their aid, and found a great pig, which a man was trying in vain to drive past them. He belaboured it with a stick, it squealed, and the children screamed, but they did not dare to move till they saw me, and we flew home together. Another day they had quite unconsciously a much more real cause for alarm. A man who was passing found them watching a death adder that was lying in the sun a few yards from their bower. After that the bower was abandoned for a time. I must say I never saw a death adder, which is really a deadly snake, but I have seen many diamond snakes, and black snakes with red stripes, but never at any time in the house. A gardener mowing the lawn was bitten one day, but with no serious result.

14th November. We all went to Port Macquarie to see the coolies who had been brought down from India by Messrs Friell and Sandeman, and who were living in a row of houses at the back of the store until arrangements were made for establishing them on a station in Queensland,[1] or what was then known as Darling Downs. I was surprised at their appearance and dress, or want of dress. They are of different castes. Some are copper coloured, who, I think, are the best looking, while others are quite dark and have better features. They are of different heights too, a few being very tall, and others equally diminutive. Mr Sheriff, who is in charge of them, pointed out some who are tradesmen—blacksmiths, carpenters, etc. He also made them show us their pipes, which are curious. One was a cocoanut shell carved and polished and filled with water, two tubes coming out from opposite sides. They showed us some brass and copper plates of a large size, and some small china cups. They seemed pleased to see us, and not at all disconcerted at being brought out to be stared at. Some had on scarlet caps with a gold band. A few more muslin turbans, but only one wore what I supposed to be their full dress, a white kind of jacket, and in addition to the dress worn by the rest, a long piece of muslin tied round his waist, the end coming down

---

[1] Queensland was not so named until 1859. Annabella is obviously editing her earlier diary.

over his feet. They have odd-looking shoes of coloured leather, turned up at the toes, and a buttonhole in them. Afterwards they showed us their musical instruments. There were two kinds of drums called by them "Tholuck"; one was held by a woman who sang and beat time on it. Her husband sang with her, and another man sat by with a kind of violin with three strings, on which he scraped with all his might. It is called a "Surungie". Their singing was not unpleasant. I thought the woman rather good-looking; she had the division of her hair rubbed with red paint, which at first I thought was a cut. Her toe and finger nails were also tipped with red, and she wore bracelets and earrings. Those of our party who were riding went home by Tacking Point and the beach.

22nd November. Dr and Mrs Jamack, Mr and Mrs Woodward, and the Misses Woodward called early and remained to luncheon. We afterwards walked in the garden, and I had a long talk with Miss Woodward about Parramatta and friends there. They have also been at Bathurst. They are both very agreeable, and pretty too, with beautiful eyes, the eldest serious-looking, but Miss Emily all animation.

24th November. Went to church, but were very late. The pulpit, or rather the reading desk, has been moved, and the clerk now sits in a pew beside it. We enjoyed the service and the impressive way in which Mr Woodward read and addressed himself to the congregation. There was an unpleasant interruption by one of the invalids taking a fit and having to be carried out of church. Port Macquarie was at that time still a depôt for Invalid Prisoners, and the congregation largely consisted of these men, the chain gang, soldiers and Government officials who were in charge.

Thursday, 28th November. We set out early and rode to Camden Haven River. The sun was very hot and we found that our pretty Scotch caps were not meant for shade: we might as well ride in a wig! However, we were delighted with our

---

[1] He was curate to St Thomas's Church.

expedition. We crossed Grant's Head, which juts out into the sea, and against which the waves beat loudly. At the other side there is a beautiful little valley sloping to the sea and some cattle grazing on it made it quite a pretty picture. Camden Haven River is some distance further on. I was surprised to find the entrance so narrow. However, there was a tolerably sized vessel with two masts at anchor in the basin. Here we dismounted and rested so long that we had to gallop a good part of the way home.

Saturday, 30th November. Mr Grey called, and he is delighted with Mr Woodward, but not at all pleased at his having altered the position of the pulpit in church.

Mamma has heard again from my aunt, Mrs Ranken. She writes in very low spirits. They have returned to Glen Logan, and she says her chief employment ever since has been getting things picked up out of the mud in the house, and off the grass, such as towels, sheets, and children's clothes, and having them washed in the river. They had to abandon everything in their hasty flight—all their clothes and books are completely ruined, as the water rose to the height of 4ft 10in. in the house, and left nearly a foot deep of mud. Trunks that had been placed on table for safety were floated off, and the contents scarcely recognizable; her wedding dress, originally white silk, is now of all the colours in the rainbow, a handsome brocaded and shot silk having bestowed most of its varied colouring on it.

Wednesday, 18th December. I scarcely know myself, I have been so industrious of late; in fact, we have all been equally busy. Dido has wrought wonders in the shape of a new white dress and other garments, the great thing being to have as many new things as possible for New Year's Day. She has also made herself a bustle almost as big as herself, and I, not to be outdone, have put a new width into mine. I have also made two dresses. During my uncle's absence we have dined early, and, having the house to ourselves, have sat in the veranda near the library, which is always shaded and cool. One of our party

PERIL IN THE SURF (1844)

reads aloud while the others work. Our book is *The Old Curiosity Shop*. We are deeply interested in Little Nell, and enjoy it doubly when my aunt reads. On Friday evening, the 20th, we were all called to the front of the house to look at the comet. It was very small and insignificant compared to that of last March, but we stood watching it till an envious cloud hid it from our view. We saw this comet several times afterwards, but it was never very bright. It appeared always high above our heads, and disappeared upwards.

On Monday, 23rd, my uncle returned from New England, bringing quite a numerous Christmas party, as we hoped he would do. We were all delighted to have him home again, and to see him looking so well. It rained heavily all night, and on Christmas day was still so wet we could not go to church, but after luncheon it cleared sufficiently to allow us to go to the new garden for fruit—apricots and Chinese peaches.

Thursday. We took a long ride. The beach was in splendid order for a good gallop.

On Friday the Misses Jobling came to spend a week with us. They are very nice girls, but so very tiny, the tallest scarcely five feet. Mr Graham and Mr Fenwick went for them, and all were delayed at Gooloowa by a thunderstorm, which had kept us in also. Next morning we devoted to needlework, as the rain still continued, and one read aloud. The gentlemen sent us in a splendid basket full of fruit, an attention we much appreciated. When we went down to lunch we found the party increased by the arrival of Mr Gray and his two shadows, Mr Hay and Mr Massie. Mr Archer had also arrived to stay for a few days, so we sat down a party of eighteen. It was then arranged we should go on the lake. I was excused, as I am not at all fond of boating, but joined them in a delightful ramble before dinner. The new footman, George, who has been here some weeks and is a very good servant, went off very hastily today, having appropriated a number of things, chiefly clothes from Bachelors' Hall, and distributed them as Christmas gifts.

Now I must describe as well as I can, our adventures of Sunday, 29th December 1844.—To plunge at once into the subject, as we were nearly doing into the mud, I must tell you we set out for church in the large carriage, eight ladies and Gustavus, my uncle driving. There were five gentlemen riding, but we are not allowed to ride on Sundays. Instead of turning off the old road as we have usually done of late, we went straight on, thinking that the road had been repaired, and the drains on each side cleared which led to a wooden bridge about a mile from the town. The water there had risen considerably since the formation of the dam, and the late rains had increased it. On coming in sight of the bridge the extent of water certainly looked very alarming. It was too late to turn back, unless by taking the horses out of the carriages and standing in the water. The ditches on each side were full of water which overflowed the road, and made it dangerous to turn, so my uncle determined to push through if possible. Some of the gentlemen who were riding went on before to encourage the horses.

At first I felt rather afraid, but in my anxiety to convince Dido who was in the rumble with me that there was no danger, I had almost succeeded in convincing myself, when suddenly we came to a standstill in water about eighteen inches deep, and the carriage which was leaning very much to my side seemed likely to go over. Happily, the wheels sank so deep in the mud that we soon found we had nothing to fear in that way. The question now was how we were to be got out of the carriage. It was quite evident that the horses were not able to draw it out of the mud. As soon as we stopped, Mr Patrick Mackay and Mr Archer, who were behind, cantered up to the carriage, and in so doing splashed us a great deal more than was necessary. The latter immediately dismounted and proposed that he should take us off on his horse.

Mr Patrick no doubt thought of doing the same but found his right foot so unwilling to touch the water, that he changed his mind. On looking round after seeing Dido safely mounted on Mr Archer's great horse, I saw that Mr Hugh had pulled off his coat and carried Gustavus to a place of safety, and was now carrying off Miss Jobling in triumph. I could not help laughing, though the spectacle we presented was far from amusing. The carriage, of course, was the most prominent object, leaning very much to one side, and entirely surrounded by water, my uncle standing in his place on the box encouraging his horses to be steady. Margaret sat beside him pale and anxious, the party inside laughing and bewailing their fate in the one breath. Presently Mr Hugh returned, and my aunt resigned herself quietly to his care. Meantime Mr Archer had brought back his charger, but could not persuade him to go near enough to the carriage. Miss Ann B—— from the rumble was handing books and parasols to Mr Patrick, which he took the first opportunity of replacing in the carriage. That young lady after a great scramble was placed on the saddle, and the restless steed led through the water, and in her eagerness to dismount she nearly tumbled off backwards. Mr Patrick took little Gordy off before him on Cupid. Mamma and Margaret were now the only two left.

The former was with some difficulty put on horseback, for the creatures would scarcely approach the carriage, and Mr Archer's frantic entreaties that she would place her hand in his foot, did not convey to her mind that he wished her to place her foot on his hand so that he might help her into the saddle. Mr Hugh carried Margaret, hard work, for she is tall, and in addition to the difficulty of walking in water knee deep, he sank over his ankles in mud at every step.

And there on the rising ground at the safe side of the bridge sat Mr James enjoying the scene amazingly, and, as my uncle said, looking like the grand Turk smoking with an air of calm indifference and saying to himself, "It's all fate; if they are to stick in the mud, there they will stick; if not, they'll get out without me." All being safely landed, my uncle desired us to move on. We waited only to see him urge his horses to make one more effort, but they could not move, and the poor creatures seemed to be thoroughly subdued and disheartened. We had a hot, dusty walk of a mile and a half to the settlement, and met a party of men on their way to my uncle's assistance. The gentlemen who were with us turned back with them to see the carriage drawn safely out of the mud. Some of our party had ridden over to ask for aid, and we heard afterwards that the men we met had been brought out of church, so no wonder that when we entered after the sermon had commenced every one thought it their duty to stare at us. No doubt we looked rather remarkable with fiery red faces and dishevelled hair, our white dresses crumpled and bespattered with mud.

On coming out of church it was arranged that we should walk till the carriage overtook us, which we did, taking the route by the long bridge; but our chapter of accidents was not yet complete, for Mr Fenewick put Gustavus on his horse, which he led, but forgot to take further notice of him, being too much engaged paying attention to Miss Jobling. The consequence was that Gustavus fell off and sprained his wrist. We had scarcely recovered from the alarm we were thrown into by this accident when, fortunately, the carriage overtook us.

It was three o'clock before we found ourselves safely at home, the distance from the church being quite seven miles. The horses behaved beautifully, but my uncle declares he will never have the large carriage out again without four horses. I think it is as well he had only two on this occasion, as four would probably have doubled our difficulties.

Chapter

7

"THE STOCKMAN'S LAST BED" 1845, 1846

I SHALL PASS briefly over the next two years, 1845-46. The country was still in a very depressed state; transportation had practically ceased, and everywhere the want of labour was severely felt. An emigration scheme had been started by Mrs Chisholm, an energetic and philanthropic lady, who took much personal trouble in carrying out the good work, but at first only single female emigrants were brought out by her. Many people who had once been prosperous had lost all they possessed and were leaving the colony in disgust or despair, others saw a dawning prospect of better times and braced themselves up to make a fresh start.

Nothing of any great personal interest happened in our own immediate circles, but there were, of course, events of more or less social importance in the district and neighbourhood.

Early in 1845 Mr Friell married Miss Emily Woodward, and they went at once to live in Sydney. Mrs and Miss Stevens left Hamilton and went to Sydney, where soon after the latter was married to Mr Hay. Mr Hay was succeeded in Port Macquarie by Lieut. G. J. de Winton, a very fascinating young man, handsome and clever. Fortunately his arrival was accompanied by the announcement of his engagement, so as far as I know no hearts were broken, especially as he spoke quite openly of "the

Adorable Fanny", whom eventually he married. His cousin also married another "Adorable Fanny", which sometimes caused a little confusion. Mr Wright succeeded Mr de Winton, but we preferred our little friend Mr Montgomerie to any of his brother officers.

During these two years we improved our acquaintance with many of our more distant friends and neighbours, and their families, who, like ourselves, were rapidly growing up. Major and Mrs Kemp came from the Macleay, and brought a son and daughter. Mr Oaks and his sister came also from the Macleay, and Mr and Miss Ducat—the latter brought with them sometimes their aunt, Miss Gray, a delightful old Scotch lady, so bright and sympathetic; we loved to hear her quaint speech. We always breakfasted rather late; one morning my uncle said to her, "I am afraid you must be very hungry." "No, no, Major," she replied, "I'm not to say hungry, but I'm just appeteezed." Mrs Scott, a friend and neighbour of the Ducats, came occasionally with them; she sang charmingly, and we all liked her very much, but she had a large family, and could not easily leave home. Mr Archibald Boyd paid a farewell visit to the Lake before leaving the Colony. He was most agreeable, and a great conversationalist. He told many good and amusing stories.

In July 1846 the new race-course was opened. I believe the races were fairly good—they certainly were well attended. We had a very gay time, and enjoyed ourselves immensely. The house was quite full, and my aunt gave a dance, to which everyone within a distance of fifty miles came.

I think it was during the previous summer we had the pleasure of carrying out the long promised visit to Tilbuster, which is situated in a rich agricultural district about thirty miles from Port Macquarie. We crossed the river in the punt at Blackman's Point, and rode through Roland's Plains, where there are many farms and pretty homesteads. I had never before seen so much ground under cultivation. The house at Tilbuster is small but very pretty, some of the rooms panelled with cedar. The place had a special interest in being my aunt's "marriage portion", given by the Government, and named after her old home in Surrey. In 1839, and for some years after, a law was in force giving a small grant to parties marrying with the intention of settling in the Colony, but not obliging them to live on the land. The manager lived in the house at Tilbuster, and under him in the old days were a large number of convict servants who farmed the land and grew the wheat, maize, and hay required for the contracts taken by my uncle to supply the various Government officials, soldiers, and invalids then resident in Port Macquarie, also a large number of convicts who were employed in making the road to New England, and other work.

A few years before our visit to Tilbuster a great disaster befell that flourishing establishment. I have heard my uncle say it was the first of the many misfortunes which followed. The crops had all been gathered in, the barns were full, and stacks of wheat and hay stood ready to be threshed or carted away, when a terrific thunderstorm broke over the farm, and the barn was struck by lightning, the whole of the out-buildings and their

"We had the pleasure of carrying out the long promised visit to Tilbuster."

"THE STOCKMAN'S LAST BED" (1845, 1846)

contents were destroyed by fire, the cottage only being saved. The following year crops failed throughout the whole Colony, prices rose, and contracts that had been made when the barns were full had to be carried out at a very serious loss. But all this was in the past and did not trouble us at the moment, as no trace of the fire remained. There was a charming view from the house, which was situated on rising ground, and our one annoyance was that some people insisted that the place we looked at was prettier than Tilbuster. No doubt it looked prettier from Tilbuster, than Tilbuster looked from it, and we could not agree as to whether the view from or the view of a place constituted its beauty. I say the former.

That autumn Mr John Macleay, a cousin of my aunt's, came to stay at the Lake. He was very delicate, and it was hoped that his health would improve in the fine air and pleasant surroundings. Unfortunately this hope was not realized, and, as a sea voyage was recommended, he sailed for London. Our friend, Mr Gunn, went with him. Poor Mr Macleay died during the voyage. We were all sorry. He had interested us greatly; he was so gentle and handsome. I spent many an hour reading aloud to him.

In 1846 our friend Mr William Mackenzie went to China, and his partner, Mr Robert Graham, married Miss Grey, and took his bride to the Cape, where they settled permanently, but before that Colonel Grey had brought both his daughters to stay with us. I shall never forget Maria's first visit. She was then about sixteen, and the prettiest little creature imaginable, with beautiful grey eyes fringed with long black eyelashes, and over-arched by eyebrows black and shapely, while her hair hung in masses of flaxen curls. She was barely five feet in height, and when she spoke her face became radiant with smiles and dimples. We all succumbed at once to her many charms. That evening she wore a dress of pale green challis, with a pattern on it of large bunches of flowers, and made with a short waist, and full short sleeves—anything so quaint and pretty I never saw. She was like a picture, and so unconscious of her own attractiveness.

After dinner the sisters sang to us very sweetly. Maria sang a perfect second, though she did not know a note of music. Both the girls were good French scholars and well read, as Colonel Grey possessed a good library. Their education had been carried on under his direction, assisted by an accomplished and eccentric gentleman, who for some time employed himself as tutor to their brothers. Bessy wrote some pretty poems, not without merit, and together they composed a parody on what was then a very favourite song, "The Last Whistle"—which they called "The Stockman's Last Bed". I here give a copy of it.

THE STOCKMAN'S LAST BED

TUNE—THE LAST WHISTLE

Whether stockman or not, for a moment give ear,
Poor Jack's breathed his last, and no more shall we hear
The crack of his whip or his steed's lively trot,
His clear go-ahead and his jingling quart-pot.
He rests where the wattles their sweet fragrance shed,
And tall gum-trees shadow the stockman's last bed.

When drafting one day he was gored by a cow;
Alas, cried poor Jack, it's all up with me now;
I'll no more return to my saddle again,
Or bound like a wallaby over the plain.
I'll rest where the wattles their sweet fragrance shed,
And tall gum-trees shadow the stockman's last bed.

My whip must be silent, my steed he will mourn,
My dogs look in vain for their master's return.
Unknown and forgotten, unheeded I'll die,
Save Australia's dark sons none will know where I lie.
I'll rest where the wattles their sweet fragrance shed
And tall gum-trees shadow the stockman's last bed.

Oh! stranger if ever on some future day,
When after a herd you may happen to stray,
Where lone and forgotten poor Jack's bones are laid
Far, far from the land where in childhood he played,
Tread lightly where wattles, their sweet fragrance shed,
And tall gum-trees shadow the stockman's last bed.

"THE STOCKMAN'S LAST BED" (1845, 1846)

But it was as a "Siffleuse" that Maria most distinguished herself and astonished us. In these days she might have rivalled the lady of American fame, but when we were girls, no lady was supposed ever to do such a manly thing as to whistle, so perhaps our having to listen to her with closed doors or in the open air when none of our elders were near, added a charm. Her brother Charlie was equally accomplished, and when they whistled a duet together it was inexpressively charming, unlike any music I ever heard, so thrillingly clear and effective.

In the winter of 1846 my cousin, Nancy Macleod, was married to Mr George Sharpe. She wished me to be one of her brides-maids, but I could not go to Sydney at the time. The family lived in Cumberland Place, where later on I paid them a pleasant visit. At the entrance door the house appeared a modest two-storied dwelling. From the windows at the opposite side, there was a most extensive view over lower George Street and Campbell's Wharf to the harbour. We looked into a large garden with fine orange-trees, in it stood a house which was then occupied by Mr John Campbell and his sister, we seemed very high above it. I suppose all this has been swept away long ago, and the garden built over. I did not see Mr Macleod, who had returned to Gipp's Land, where he was building a house at Bairnsdale, to which he shortly after took his large family.

It was at this time I paid my first visit to Tivoli, and became acquainted with Captain and Mrs Dumaresq and their family, my loved and valued friends. Mrs Dumaresq was my aunt's sister; their father, Mr Alexander Macleay (formerly Colonial Secretary), was then Speaker of the Legislative Council. A large family party went to the opening ceremony while I was at Tivoli. It is interesting now to remember that we saw Mr Robert Lowe, afterwards Lord Sherbrooke, take his seat as member for St Vincent. He had previously been nominated a member by Sir George Gipps, but had resigned, and was afterwards elected.

Chapter

8

WHEN THE GOVERNOR CAME 1847

W E HAD A VERY MERRY Christmas time 1846-47. My uncle brought a party from New England with him; we also had the Messrs MacKay and two Messrs M'Douall staying with us, and the usual visitors came from Port Macquarie to dine. We rode almost daily. Dido has a delightful new horse called Dandy; no name could be more appropriate for he is such a gay, prancing creature—a bright chestnut. Margaret is faithful to her Black Prince; I am devoted to Cupid; Tipoo Saib rules over Gordy, and Gustavus has abandoned Don Juan in favour of Tremaine.

We did not fail to welcome in the New Year, but early that morning the steamer left Port Macquarie, and with it went most of our guests.

After that we had Major and Mrs Kemp, Colonel and Mrs Gray, and Mr and Mrs Dunsmuir to stay, and a variety of people at lunch. One day Mr Raafe and Mr Vivian Cox joined the party at dinner; they had been on the lake all day taking observations. Mr Raafe is full of a grand plan for turning the lake into a harbour,[1] the entrance to be from Cati Creek. Considering that the channel is now entirely filled up with a wide belt of sand, there is some reason to fear a bar, but he proposes

[1] The relative water levels make this project impossible.

to turn the River Hastings from its present course and bring it into the lake, which would require a canal only three miles long. This scheme might answer. Thirty feet more depth of water than there is at present is the quantity required, but a sanguine castle-building imagination can easily picture its completion. Fancy a fleet at anchor in our peaceful lake, the swans with their sombre plumage driven off by gay little pleasure boats, all softer sounds disturbed by the splashing of the steamers' paddles and the tinkling of their bells, not to mention the horrid noises of a populous town, which is to spring up as if by magic on its banks. Adieu to the acres of reeds which will be submerged and hide for ever their diminished heads, adieu also to the beauty of this lovely spot which would be quite marred by such improvements. The good town of Port Macquarie has my best wishes that it may still continue the Metropolis of this district, and I think my good wishes will be fulfilled.

We enjoyed Mr and Mrs Dunsmuir's visit very much, though it began very unfortunately. The day after their arrival he was thrown from his horse and dislocated his shoulder. We were greatly alarmed at the moment, but by the end of the week he was so much better that it was arranged we should go to Tilbuster for a few days. However, this had to be given up, as a heavy rainfall caused the rivers to rise so rapidly it was impossible to cross them. Happily we had not started. Mrs Dunsmuir was very young, very girlish and pretty, full of fun, and much amused at her own importance as a married lady. One day we rode to Hamilton, then occupied by Mr Salway. The house has a deep veranda and wide passage through it. It is situated on the bank of the river Hastings below Blackman's Point, and, being so near the sea, the water is brackish and rises and falls with the tide. There is a fine vineyard, with a good variety of grapes. One kind was very large, and tasted rather like passion-fruit. Another day we went round by the beach, Tacking Point, and the Settlement—a charming ride—which our friends much admired.

On 22nd January 1847 our pleasant party broke up. My uncle and Gustavus, Colonel and Mrs George Grey, Mr and Mrs Dunsmuir left for Sydney by the steamer. Maria and I went to see them off, and found ourselves in quite a crowd. All the ladies of Port Macquarie had come on board to say goodbye to Mrs Friell. All the gentlemen were there, of course. The trades people had taken just a few minutes' holiday to see what was going on. All the nurses and children were irresistibly attracted to the wharf, and the idlers, of course, had nothing else to do. Mrs Friell sat in state on deck, adorned with many jewels, ear-rings, chains, etc. Captain Gordon amused me by whispering "She'll soon unship all that." We were very sorry indeed to say goodbye to Colonel Grey, who has been offered a Government appointment in the north. It is sad for him to be, as it were, beginning the world again and going he scarcely knows where. Port Curtis is, I believe, his destination, but very little of a satisfactory nature is known of this new settlement. The first people who went to it returned long ago, as they could not find a sufficient supply of wood and water. Colonel Barney has been appointed Governor or Commandant. Mrs Grey in the meantime remains at Huntington with the rest of the family. Before this our good friend Dr Stacey had left the district, much to our regret, taking with him his large family. He went to Newcastle, where he practised for several years very successfully. His eldest daughter was an extremely pretty girl. The eldest son stayed often at the Lake: he went to India with horses.

In February we heard from my uncle, who was still in Sydney, that it had been arranged that he was to accompany Sir Charles Fitzroy (the new governor) and party on their proposed tour to Beardie Plains, the Peel River, and New England, and to arrive here with them, via Yarrows, about 28th February, by which time it was expected that Lady Mary Fitzroy, Dr and Mrs Dawson,[1] and Colonel Mundy would have arrived by steamer from Sydney. We heard of their arrival

[1] Dr W. Dawson was Principal Medical Officer to the colony. He arrived in 1840.

WHEN THE GOVERNOR CAME (1847)

at Newcastle, but that the weather was then so extremely bad it was doubtful if they could carry out their journey: finally it was abandoned, and the whole party returned to Sydney. It was afterwards decided that all should come to Port Macquarie by steamer about 1st March, and the Governor with a party of gentlemen start from Lake Innes to New England, via Yarrows, leaving Lady Mary at the Lake.

On the morning of 14th February we were much excited by the arrival of a messenger from Port Macquarie to say the *Maitland* was outside the bar, all her colours flying, and no doubt the Governor was on board. We were filled with dismay, for he was not expected till March, and we were expecting a variety of things for use or ornament during their visit, and last, though not least, Mr Tozer had not yet gone to Sydney to choose the champagne for the luncheon which was to be given to his Excellency. But all is well that ends well. Aunt Barbara Macleay and Mr Wm Macleay arrived with my uncle, and we have all been very merry and busy completing the various preparations. We have been half buried in curtains, and rejoice now at seeing them grace their respective windows. The curtains, I may say, are all made of clear book muslin, the hems bound or lined with glazed calico of different colours in each room. My cousins have given up their room, and been moved into our pretty schoolroom, and I am glad to say the smell of paint in the long passages is fast disappearing.

Wednesday, 3rd March 1847. Dear Gordy's twelfth birthday. I had scarcely time to wish her many happy returns of the day I was in such haste to gather fresh flowers, and was still busy with them when a messenger arrived to say the carriage was coming up the road, but as he had started from Port Macquarie the moment the steamer had safely crossed the bar, it was nearly an hour before they appeared. The party from Sydney consisted of his Excellency, Sir Charles Fitzroy, who is immensely tall and stout, and reminds us of our old friend, Mr Wm Mackenzie; Lady Mary, who is also very tall and stout, and has but slight remains of the good looks for which she was remarkable in her youth, when in Ireland with her father, the Duke of Richmond, then Lord Lieutenant; Mr George Fitzroy,[1] their son, who is tall and slight and very good-looking; Colonel Mundy, Adjutant General, a gentlemanlike looking little man, and Dr and Mrs Dawson. The former we had all seen before, and liked extremely; no doubt we shall be equally pleased with her. The whole now form a party of eighteen at breakfast. The dinner party consisted, in addition to those in the house, of Mr Woodward, Mr Wright, Dr Gamack, Mr Grey, Mr Massie, and Mr Taylor. Mr Grey sat at the head of the table, Mr M'Kay at the foot, it being the fashion in these days for the lady and gentleman of the house to sit at the sides (in the centre), with the chief guests at either hand. We danced for a short time, and then went to our rooms, but not at once to bed, for I put on my dressing gown and went in search of water melon (not to the garden), which we thoroughly enjoyed.

Thursday, 4th March 1847. To our great joy was as fine as the day could be. We spent the morning in the drawing-room end of the veranda, where Lady Mary has established herself with her work. She is most industrious, and is now preparing for the annual fancy bazaar for the School of Industry, which is to be held on or about the Queen's Birthday. She has enlisted us all in her service, and declared she would not have come down to breakfast yesterday, but that she wanted to be beforehand with Mrs Dawson who is also collecting for a stall, and who she heard was not to appear till after breakfast. I am making a pincushion cover in imitation Brussels lace, which should be handsome. Such knitting, crocheting, and work of every kind was never seen! We are threatened with two conflicting manias, one for fancy work, the other for the Polka—a new dance, for not to know it "argues yourself unknown". We are to learn it at once, and Mrs Dawson has kindly offered to be our teacher. She is most good-natured and such a stout little woman, all full skirts and stiff petticoats—this too is a

[1]George W. Fitzroy acted as secretary to his father.

new fashion. Our visitors are rather shocked at our primitive style of dress, especially as Margaret and I are so tall, so we have written for a supply of stiff muslin, and Lady Mary has sent for her polka music.

Our dinner party today consisted of Messrs Fenwick, Massie, Grey, Major Kemp, Capt. Wauch, Briggs and Geary, Rev. Mr Purvis (P), and Mr Bigney (R.C.). We had never seen Capt. Briggs before, though he has long been a settler on the M'leay, and has two sons and a daughter almost grown up; he is a tall, fine-looking man. Strange to say, he is an old friend of Mrs Dawson's, who knew him years ago in the West Indies, and was surprised to meet him here, and to find the slender ensign had changed into so stout and grave-looking a Captain. The Governor and most of the gentlemen went to Port Macquarie today. I believe an address was presented and all that, but I have heard no particulars. Mr Mackay drove with Lady Mary, and my aunt and Maria and I rode with Mrs Dawson, who rides well, but had not been or horseback for eight years.

Friday, 5th March. Lady Mary, I am glad to say, is much better. She has been an invalid for some time, and yesterday was not well. Mrs Fenwick and Mrs Kemp called and stayed to luncheon. Mrs Purvis kindly brought us out the music of the polka, and when the others went to ride I remained at home to learn to play it, and to write my journal. They returned at dark, delighted with their ride, as the beach was in such good order. Mr Grey, the Messrs Oaks, Halloran, Freeman, Goram, Dr Fattorini and the Rev. Mr Currie dined here. Strange to say I had never seen Dr Fattorini before, though at one time he was a constant guest here, but I seemed to recognize him at once and danced the first quadrille with him. We are still indefatigable dancers, and ended the evening by trying to learn the polka. I played while Mrs Dawson and Mr Fitzroy danced. I wished I had an eye in the back of my head, as it was all lost on me where I was sitting. Lady Mary was kind enough to shew me the proper time, and when her books come we are to learn and to copy some pretty polkas from them. Mrs Dawson is also to get hers, and teach every lady here to dance, so I begin to agree with Colonel Mundy, who says it is a kind of madness, and when it first appeared in England old and young were alike infected by it. He told us that a fashionable dancing mistress (I forget her name) had made thousands in one season by teaching it.

Saturday, 6th March. We were to have gone on the lake this morning, but it proved very warm, and, as the gentlemen wished to keep themselves cool, it was deferred. The Governor, my uncle, Dr Dawson, Colonel Mundy, and Mr Fitzroy went to Port Macquarie about one o'clock to attend a public dinner (or luncheon) given to his Excellency. We did not envy them. Aunt Barbara went to drive with Lady Mary, and the rest of us adjourned to the dancing-room with Mrs Dawson, and there polked till I was dreadfully tired, though I was also chief musician; then we took a comfortable nap for an hour, after which I went out to gather flowers, as we must each have a bouquet, and Sir Charles cannot dine without a fresh buttonhole. Lady Mary is also very fond of flowers so I tried my skill again after my lesson from Mr Fitzroy and succeeded very well. He presented me with a miniature broom of various coloured flowers, which I told him I thought a poor compliment after Dido's remark when he was making it, that "surely he meant it for a lady with monstrous hands", and indeed he was not far wrong in bestowing it on me. Lady Mary has most beautiful hands and feet, and always wears rings, which reminds me that Maria Grey has brought down a ring to shew to us, which belongs to Robert the Bruce. The Earl of Stair gave it to her grandfather. It is the most clumsy thing imaginable, a large turquoise set in gold. We were to have dined earlier and supped with the gentlemen. However, they returned before dinner was announced and joined us. I have been trying to get some account of their entertainment, but no one gets further than Colonel Mundy's speech in which he declared he was half tempted to exchange his cocked hat for one of cabbage-tree, and his sword for sheep shears! Mr Wright who returned

thanks for the ladies muttered it all to himself, and Mr Grey, who was in the chair, proved himself to be so unaccustomed to public speaking (though he did not say so) that I shall make no further remark.

Sunday, 7th March. My aunt's birthday, but as I was not able to appear at breakfast I did not wish her many happy returns till I was saying goodnight. Two carriages full went to church. It was excessively hot. In the afternoon Mr Woodward held a service here. He preached in the drawing-room at an open French window, and the people who came had forms in the veranda, but I doubt if they heard a word he said. His text was from Genesis, "And Joseph was Governor over the land." He concluded by saying that he had arrived in this Colony in gloomy times, which he was glad to know were now brightening, and he trusted that the Colony would prosper and that a Joseph had arisen among us, and, "May God bless his Excellency the Governor of this territory" (not in good taste). Mr Taylor and Mr Massie called.

Monday, 8th March. I may say I dressed in the dark, for it was a dull morning and we were all down by six o'clock to see the gentlemen before they started on their journey to New England. As they did not go off at once, we had time to observe, if not admire, their bush costumes. The Governor wore a very light coat, and I had the honour of tying on his veil of blue purse silk (netted by Miss Icely, and the best thing possible for keeping off flies, as it is so cool and light). Mr Fitzroy appeared with a great green veil, wrapped round a tall white hat. I thought it must be a kind of mourning, a green willow I had heard of, but green crape never. Its size is admirable.

> Contrived a double debt to pay.
> Curtains by night, to save his eyes by day.

He wore long boots with a great piece cut out under the knee, and dark cornered unutterables, a stable jacket and waistcoat of small black and white check, a coloured shirt and neckerchief, and in this behold a bushman's costume of the year 1847! I wish I could have made a sketch such as Dido has got from Colonel Mundy. It is taken from his bedroom window with Campden Haven etc. in the distance, but in the foreground is Mr Fitzroy fast asleep. We were all anxious to secure such a treasure, so it was put up for auction unreservedly to the highest bidder, each one to be in ignorance of the other's offer, and Mrs Dawson to decide. (Age before honesty.) I offered a pen-wiper, Maria a pincushion, Margaret a watch-guard, Dido a knitted purse (winner), Gordy a watch-pocket. We were in despair, but I have won a "philipe" from him, and mean to insist upon its payment. Sir Charles and Colonel Mundy drove as far as Thrumster. They all stop at Yarrows tonight. It was dull and cold but no rain. In the evening we had the Polka, and then cards.

Tuesday, 9th March. It rained and so there was no going out. Lady Mary gave us a long and interesting account of the earthquake in Antigua, which took place while Sir Charles was Governor there. She has promised to send for a newspaper that was printed at the time, and which gives, she says, a most faithful account of the event. She told us of a lady, a friend of hers, who had a most miraculous escape. She had been for some time a great invalid, and was still confined to her own room, where she was sitting in her dressing gown and slippers, when her attendant, a coloured man, rushed in and pulled her out of her easy chair, which almost instantly sank through the floor, and the whole of that part of the house fell in ruins. The lady escaped from a window by a ladder put up to it for her, by a man who fortunately was near. She scrambled down, and with difficulty reached an open space under the shade of some trees. In a few minutes what had so lately been her comfortable home became a mass of ruins. People who visited the spot afterwards could scarcely imagine how she had made her escape and that she did not suffer from the fright and excitement she had gone through. Her husband, Sir Robert, who was in the town when the shock took place, instantly mounted his horse and galloped to his country house, which he that morning had left in beauty and fancied secure, to find now only scattered heaps of rubbish. You may imagine his dismay till a kind neighbour told him of his wife's safety and led him to where she had taken refuge.

Thursday, 11th March. We had a delightful pic-nic at the beach in honour of it being the anniversary of Lady Mary's wedding day. The carriage and four started about two o'clock with her Ladyship, my Aunt Barbara, and Dr Dawson. We were glad he could stay long enough to be of the party. Mamma, Mrs Dawson and we four girls, Mr Mackay, and Mr Macleay followed on horseback. I was astonished when we arrived at the beach to find on the bank overlooking it a long table spread with an excellent and substantial cold lunch, to which was added hot currie and potatoes. The cart had been sent down early and the whole party looked quite formidable. We found those who had driven down seated on the bank admiring the wide sea view which is magnificent; near them was drawn up the carriage with the four horses in the background. There was a fire, round which hovered the cook, radiant with smiles at his own importance; beside him was his Sunday coat which he slipped on whenever he came forward, not that he was required to help to wait as we had four footmen, two of our own, Lady Mary's, and Dr Dawson's. Her maid and Christina were also there, and as we rode up a man appeared from a clump of trees where I noticed three others reclining, helpers we supposed, but they nearly caused me to fall from my horse, for what with the surprise of coming suddenly on them, and the fluttering of flags, poor Cupid took fright and wheeled round so suddenly that I was thankful to find myself still on the saddlle and not under his feet. After lunch we had a canter on the beach to try if it was firm enough for the carriage to go down, but Elton, the coachman, who is a splendid and experienced driver, thought it would be wise to wait for a few days when the tide would suit better. Finally we rode home, and on as far as the race-course where we saw some horses galloping. In the evening we varied our amusement by a game at fright which I won, after enduring much anxiety of mind in case the bright and beautiful penny for which we were playing should escape from my greedy grasp.

On Friday all the young people except myself and Mrs Dawson rode to Blackman's Point to invite Miss Jobbling, who came next day with her brother—a very nice boy, but shy, and nothing would induce him to be presented to Lady Mary. It was his eighteenth birthday, and Mrs Macleay's, in honour of which we had decorated the breakfast table with flowers. Mrs Freeman called with her son and daughter, the boy a compound of awkwardness without bashfulness; such wonderful bows he made, and why should he fear Lady Mary? The Queen had visited the Bluecoat School when he was there, and had said to him, "What is your name, little boy?" " 'Frank Freeman, ma'am,' said I," and well might he be proud! Dr Dawson left for Sydney. Mamma drove to Port Macquarie with him, and went to see Mrs Gorman, who is ill. On the return of the carriage Gordy was presented with a doll, Aunt Barbara with a parcel of sweets and two mouse-traps. Who they came from I am not at liberty to tell, for the truth is we do not know.

Sunday, 14th, was dear Gustavus's ninth birthday. He is at school at Stroud.[1] We drank his health after dinner in addition to that of the travellers, which has been our toast for the last week.

Monday, 15th, proved a delightful day, which we were glad of, as it had been arranged that Lady Mary was to have a drive on the beach. The tide answered early, so we set off immediately after lunch, and she enjoyed it extremely, having no fear, but when my uncle heard of their exploits he was very angry, as it really was dangerous to take four spirited horses unaccustomed to the sea and the surf. Our ponies dash along in any state of the tide or the weather, being well used to the beach. The whole party were to have ridden today, but some of the ponies were not to be found. Mrs Dawson had to take mamma's favourite Duchess, but did not like her, and came

[1] The schoolhouse still exists.

back from the bridge. Mr Grey, Capt. Briggs, and Mr Wright accompanied the others to Tacking Point.

Tuesday, 16th March. The drawing-room has the appearance of a school of industry. Lady Mary is our leader, and has finished two work bags already. She sits in what we call the flirting chair, a work table before her covered with gay silks and wools. Mrs Dawson generally occupies the other side of the chair, and is busy now with a crochet antimacassar. Aunt Barbara and Margaret are busy at a frame working a gay piece for a cushion. Mamma is working a bag, Dido a purse, Annabella a pincushion, Gordy a collar, and Aunt Margaret occasionally sits down with her netting. The gentlemen sometimes condescend to look in, but at present they are quite occupied boating. In the evening we continue our polka lessons, but as I am musician, and we still have only one tune, I am not making much progress in either accomplishment.

Wednesday, 17th March. Mrs Wauch and her two daughters

". . . a work table
before her covered with gay silk."

WHEN THE GOVERNOR CAME (1847)

arrived before luncheon, all looking prettier than ever. It is not flattering her to say that she looks like their elder sister. Mrs Wauch left, but the girls are to remain. Our travellers were expected this evening, and we rode past Thrumster thinking we might meet them, but were disappointed. Miss Wauch drew a sketch of our party next morning. She uses her pencil with much freedom, and her sketches are clever and spirited, though the likenesses are not good. Invitations have been issued for an evening party here next Friday, which we expect to enjoy very much. Mrs Dawson is in despair about her mosquitoes bites; she really has suffered much from them. Her arms would be a feast for a cannibal, they are so plump, and parboiled by this time by constantly dipping them into hot water. We have never been so annoyed by mosquitoes before, and suppose they are attracted to the drawing-room by the lights, the windows being constantly open and the room full of people.

Thursday, 18th March. Mamma and Mrs Dawson were just setting off with Lady Mary to Port Macquarie, when an express arrived from my uncle ordering the carriage to be sent to Thrumster to meet them, and saying that Sir Charles had sprained his ankle in New England, which, of course, we were very sorry to hear. Later on Lady Mary and Mrs Dawson drove to Thrumster, and before sunset the whole party had returned, but without the escort we had expected from New England. The Governor did not appear at dinner. He must have suffered great pain having his foot so long hanging in the stirrup. Mr Fitzroy also has met with an accident. The horse he was riding threw up its head and struck him so hard that he fell off quite stunned. His teeth were loosened and his lips swelled, which is slightly disfiguring, but will soon be all right. They say it is quite cold in New England, and they had large fires night and morning. We were delighted to have Maria Grey back. She rode down with my uncle, and came up to the advance party just in time to see his Excellency get into a gig they had borrowed for his comfort, and out of which he had been most unceremoniously thrown by the horse stumbling. It is marvellous that he was not hurt. He seems an excellent traveller and takes all things very coolly. The steamer arrived at Port Macquarie early this morning. We were surprised when the letters and parcels appeared, as all eyes were watching a steamer near Camden Haven, which was thought to be the *Maitland*. Lady Mary has got her music books, and played us several charming polkas. There was also a large assortment of silk, wools, etc., for various members of the family, and Mrs Dawson has received a large portmanteau which contained, among other matters, an assortment of stiff petticoats. Among the arrivals by the steamer were Mr Paterson and family—seventeen in number, including Mrs Norman M'Leod and her two children. I shall be so glad to see them. She is to spend a month or two in Port Macquarie. The weather continued wet to our dismay, and I never heard heavier rain than fell all night.

Friday, 19th, was at least tolerably fine. We spent the morning getting our dresses in order, tacking robes to them the same as we had at the last large evening party, but trimmed with steel beads and gimp instead of flowers, trimming gloves, etc., etc. We young people dined in the dancing room in the middle of the day, and dinner was laid there for twelve at seven o'clock, then it was converted into a refreshment room with tea and coffee, punch and negus, cakes, etc. The dining-room carpet was taken up, and chairs placed at the top of the room for the Governor and Lady Mary, which left quite enough room for the dancers, as the room is rather long. Our only fear was that some tall persons might knock their heads against the chandelier, a handsome new one, for which the room is rather low. I danced with Col. Mundy, Mr Fitzroy, Mr Macleay, and some other pleasant partners. Then I fell a victim to others, four dances did I go through with Mr Oaks, and might have imagined myself engaged in a serious flirtation, only he was married last August. Mr Ducat took me to supper; he only received his invitation at eleven o'clock, and rode forty miles to be present. Mrs Freeman sat opposite, and was most

162

amusing in her remarks. The supper was laid in the veranda next to the drawing-room, and was completely closed in with strong canvas, and the table laid from end to end. Everything was excellent, and set out with the greatest taste. The Governor retired immediately after supper, and Dr Gamack examined his ankle, which he pronounced to be severely bruised and sprained.

He must have suffered a great deal of pain from it, but he was most pleasant to everyone during the evening, and to my amusement, I may say confusion, complimented me on our expertness in making up our late importation from Sydney, meaning the stiff petticoats, which had been got for the occasion, and in which we had been pronounced so sadly deficient. Fashionable people seem now to think they cannot put on too many, and some wear hair cloth bustles. They say the proper criterion is to see your bustle when you look over your shoulder. Lady Mary wore a white dress with blue stripes round her skirt as high as her knee, and blue ornaments, and looked very well. Mrs Dawson shone forth in white book muslin with a tunic skirt trimmed with lace and roses. We kept the dance up till three o'clock. We had Helen and Jessie Paterson, chaperoned by their sister Mrs Norman M'Leod, the very Agnes of former days, looking as young and pretty as when we were her bridesmaids nearly three years ago. Mrs Taylor, we thought, was very pretty.

On Saturday our party began to disperse, Capt. Waugh sent for his daughters, and Mr Taylor came for his wife, bringing his children with him. It was arranged we should ride to Blackman's Point that we might show it to our Sydney friends, but we started too late, and Mrs Dawson was afraid to be out by moonlight. After dinner we danced and I played a polka, the very last and I have never yet seen it danced.

Sunday we did not go to church. Sir Charles had an easy chair placed in the veranda near his dressing-room. A table and sofa were also brought out, and we all visited him there. His foot was very painful. I gathered some figs for him in the afternoon, and sat with him while the others went to the lake.

Monday 22nd March. Our visitors left. We accompanied them to Port Macquarie, as the Governor had kindly asked for us, and we were glad to escort him; but after we joined the main road were in dread of meeting an escort from the town, in which case we were to take another road. Happily the horsemen did not appear till we reached the Mound, so all was well. We said goodbye in the steamer, and there was great cheering as she moved from the wharf. That, and Mr Wright's gallant array of soldiers so astonished my pony that his behaviour quite frightened me, but we made our way quite safely to Fort Fitzroy (two cannons on a hillock) and from there watched the steamer cross the bar—a pretty sight, the colours all flying, and an awning all over the deck. One tiny wave broke beautifully on the deck, and now they are gone. We hope they have enjoyed their visit even half as much as we have. They have individually and collectively left a good impression here. We got home hot and hungry, and Maria declares I am always tired, hungry, or sleepy.

Wednesday, 30th March. The house has now been restored to its usual state. My aunt occupies her own rooms, and the yellow room shines forth in its own proper colours. The school-room looks quite empty, and as for me, once more sole occupant of the upper regions, I constantly oversleep myself, as there is no one to disturb me. Yesterday Dido and Mr Mackay, Cousin William and I rode to Cati Creek, which is once more running into the sea, and quite impassable. And now that the week is ended, how have we spent it? I say copying music; but there is still a great deal of work for the bazaar going on.

On Sunday my uncle returned. He went to Sydney with the Governor's party. Aunt Barbara received letters from Scotland in answer to those she sent home by Mr Gunn. It is just eleven months since he sailed from Sydney. Aunt Williamina asks her if we wear any stiff petticoats, and says she never wears less than two corded and stiff starched and one of horse-hair. We were amused to hear my uncle regretting that he had not

WHEN THE GOVERNOR CAME (1847)

ordered a supply for us when in Sydney, and mamma is commissioned to do so. I quite dread my own appearance so puffed out.

Monday, 29th March. Mrs Gamack called. Her husband is Colonial Surgeon in Port Macquarie in succession to Dr Richardson. She was formerly Mrs Cox, and an old friend of my mother. She told us they are to leave Port Macquarie on 1st May and also the Waldrons. It is thought that Mr Wright will also be moved then. The Gormans (Government Surveyor) leave soon, and Mr Purvis talks of returning to Scotland. If all this comes to pass poor Port Macquarie will be quite deserted.

Wednesday, 31st March. Mr James Mackay appeared; he has been detained by floods. He left Mr Hugh going to Fitzroy Downs, a new country further north than the Boyne. We were sorry to hear the report confirmed of the loss of the steamer *Sovereign*[1] at Brisbane. She is a complete wreck, and almost all on board have perished—among them Mr and Mrs Robert Gore and their two children. They left their eldest child with her grandmother, Mrs Baldock, about six months ago, when Mrs Gore went to the bush for the first time. Poor little girl, she little knows what she has lost; it is indeed a sad affair. Forty lives, it is said, are lost, but the particulars are not yet known. The steamer, which had been wind-bound for two or three days, was just leaving the harbour when the accident occurred. The boilers burst or some of the machinery broke down. Mrs Gore's body had been found and only one other when the account was written. A few people had been picked up alive but much injured, and conveyed at once to the hospital.

On Wednesday evening we went by appointment to see Mr Stokes. He shewed us all his cellars and appliances for wine making, which are on a much more extensive scale than we had imagined. We tasted some of the wine, which is said to be very good. There was a light wine like the palest sherry and

[1] The *Sovereign's* engines broke down as she was crossing the bar.

one very dark, both made from the same grape, which he calls the black muscat of Jura. He ferments the one with the skin on, the other is merely the juice pressed gently from the grape: it is the richer and better of the two. There was also some wine made at Hamilton by Mr Salway—horrid stuff I thought it.

At a short distance from the house there is a large store with a cellar below extending the whole size of the building. In the cellar are large casks arranged at each side, and in the centre of the upper floor there is a wide trapdoor down which these casks are lowered, but which is now practically closed and a ladder placed, down which we were invited to descend. Above were fourteen huge casks filled with this year's wine, which has only just ceased fermenting. There were also two vats for pressing the grapes in. I thought the whole place smelt horribly. The wine is racked off into clean casks about every six months, and any that does not promise well is made into brandy. I looked particularly at the still, which is the first I have ever seen. There is a small detached house for it, and another wine store which we also visited, besides a good-sized room devoted to bottled wine. We were all much interested in everything we saw. We carried off some early roses and mignonette in remembrance of our visit, and Aunt Barbara got a root of musk; she gave me a piece of it for my garden, but Isabella threw it away, and with it a bird's nest I had found when riding, the most lovely little nest I have ever seen, made chiefly of moss. It was too stupid of her.

The steamer was detained two days, I cannot say to our grief, as dear mamma and Aunt Barbara were going to Sydney in her, not to mention cousin William. On Saturday morning they left. It was a lovely day, and about one o'clock we saw the steamer passing the hill, and put up our flag to salute them.

Friday, 2nd April 1847 was dear Dido's fifteenth birthday, but being Good Friday it was decided not to keep it till today. We all rode to Tacking Point before luncheon, one of the grooms following with a basket of provisions. We met my

WHEN THE GOVERNOR CAME (1847)

"There is a small detached house for it."

uncle who had been in the settlement, and he chose a shady bank near a little creek with nice, clear water where we rested and had our lunch. Afterwards we went in search of flowers and berries, and Dido and I tried to make a sketch from the green hills at the point. Returning, we rode along the beach as far as Cati Creek, which is still running into the sea. Mr Mackay crossed it and coming back his horse got into a quicksand. Of course, it began to plunge, and to our terror he was thrown off, and for a second was completely under water. However, he managed to wade across afterwards, and though completely drenched neither horse nor rider was hurt.

Friday 9th April. The steamer arrived bringing letters from dear mamma, also a large assortment of goods for Christina, who has at last consented to wed Mr Michael Fay, and according to custom on these occasions is collecting together as many things as if she was going to sail round the world with him.

The newspapers gave long accounts of the wreck of the *Sovereign*. It took place on the 11th March in the south channel at Morton Bay, and was attended with a dreadful loss of life, forty-four persons out of fifty-four on board being drowned, among them Mr and Mrs Robert Gore whose melancholy fate has excited much sorrow and compassion even among strangers. A Mr Richard Stubbs, the only cabin passenger saved, seems to have had more than usual presence of mind, and speaks of having tried to lash two bales of wool together, a hopeless effort in the boiling surf. Mrs Gore's body and that of her eldest child were washed at once on shore and buried by the survivors in the sand, also that of a sailor, but no others were found for several days. As it was not possible to remove them Captain Wickham read the burial service over them the next day. Two poems have appeared in the Sydney newspapers on the subject of the wreck. One is particularly touching as preserving the last words of Mrs Gore, and truly in contemplating her death though attended with such awful circumstances one is almost tempted to exclaim, may my last end be like hers.

On Sunday 11th Mr Woodward preached a beautiful sermon from 1st Corinthians, xv., 51, "Behold I show you a mystery. We shall not all sleep, but we shall all be changed." Of course he referred to this sad and dreadful shipwreck.

Thursday, 15th April. Rode to Blackman's Point; quite a large party as we were joined by Messrs Massey, Salway, and Wright, who all came out to tell us about an oystering party they had been at that morning, but the only information I can give is that Mr Salway, who was the leader of the expedition, proved that the oyster bed which he prided himself upon as being known to few, was unknown to himself, and I suppose that dreading such a discovery he had provided for his friends a delicious chicken pie which happily quite contented them.

The next entry in my journal is Thursday, 28th June, more than two months. Six weeks of this time we spent in Sydney. No doubt we wrote and received many letters telling of our doings while there, but I cannot find any.
When Lady Mary Fitzroy was with us she kindly invited

Margaret and me to pay her a visit in May, and Mrs Dawson pressed us very much to stay with her. My aunt was unwilling to promise we should go, and finally Sir Charles took up the matter, and amused us very much by saying he would make a promise to come to the Lake again before they left the Colony, if we were allowed to go to the birthday ball. If not, he certainly would not come back. It was impossible to say no to this proposal, though it put sincerity to the test, and I felt it was well we did not live in the palace of truth.

In May Mr George Fitzroy sprained his ankle, and the ball was put off. My uncle, however, said we had better go to Sydney as arranged. Mamma was there, and we had other visits to pay. He seemed to think with Lady Mary that it was quite important we should "come out", an expression I had never before heard. So to Sydney we went, and our first visit was to my cousin Mrs Sharpe, who then lived at Darling Point. We stayed also at Tivoli with Mrs Dumaresq, and with Mrs Dawson, but we never got as far as Brownlow Hill,[1] and only called at Government House as the Governor was at Parramatta nearly all the time we were in Sydney.

Mrs Dawson chaperoned us to a private ball on the Queen's birthday, and to an afternoon dance on board a man-of-war. We did not go to stay with her till June, when the postponed birthday ball took place at Government House on the 18th, and was a very brilliant affair. We found dancing in a large and crowded ballroom very different to our dances at the Lake, though we had no lack of partners. Our mother was at the ball, the first and only time I ever saw her in full evening dress. She wore black velvet and white lace, and looked noticeably handsome. Margaret and I wore white book muslin dresses over many stiff petticoats, white lace berthes trimmed with white satin, and white satin sash pinned in front, and pink roses in our hair. We enjoyed ourselves very much, and remained after the ball was over to supper with the Government House party, who were very lively and amusing.

[1] The house still exists and is just outside Camden.

While we were staying with Mrs Dawson she gave a dance and a very large dinner party, at which the Governor and Lady Mary and other Government officials were present. Captain William Blyth O'Connel took me into dinner (grandson of Governor Bligh of *Bounty* fame; his wife was a sister of Mrs Robert Mackenzie). Lady O'Connel also gave a dance to which we went, and we had many other invitations but were obliged to hurry home before the end of the month.

To continue from my journal, we landed at Port Macquarie about seven in the morning on Monday, 28th June, and found the carriage waiting to take us out to the dear Lake. I was charmed to be at home again and soon the remembrance of our visit to Sydney seemed more like a dream than reality, except that dear mamma had remained there. We were absent exactly six weeks and enjoyed ourselves very much. Everyone was so kind and attentive to us, but we were disappointed in not going to Brownlow Hill, neither did we see Aunt Barbara or Uncle George. We had a very good passage from Sydney (twenty-eight hours) but then had to anchor ten hours off the bar, as we could not come in till daylight. We missed Mr James Mackay who was so kind to us on our way to Sydney. We found Miss Kemp here and her brother, also Mr Capel Smith, and the Messrs Mackay. Maria Grey and her brother came in the evening, also Mrs and the Misses Waugh, and Miss Ducat, all this preparatory to the Races, which took place the following day. I did not go as my aunt was very unwell, but our party thought them very stupid as all the horses we were interested in lost or ran away. The gentlemen, all but my uncle, went to the race dinner. Those staying here came out to join us in a dance. My aunt was better and Bruce played, as he said if his master did not go to dinner he would not go. Mrs Bruce was here too with her boy, a fine little fellow, who bids fair to play the pipes well if one can judge of the strength of his lungs by the noise he makes.

On Wednesday, 30th, we all went to the races chaperoned by Mrs Waugh. The first was a hurdle race and only two horses started and at the hurdle immediately before the stand off fell both the riders. Much to our disgust our favourite ran off and could not be caught for some time. The other was seized by half a dozen people, his rider remounted and won at his leisure. The next race was won by Dr Gamack's Phantom. We wished he had been present as his satisfaction might have enlivened us. Hector Macleod's pony Robin won a race, and Rackay cantered round for the last, no other appearing against him, and so ended the sports of the day. It seems doubtful if they will be renewed next year, as the population of the district is diminishing so rapidly and the interest taken is very little now that the novelty has worn off.

1st July. Maria Grey and her brother left this morning. All the others of our party went from the race-course, as the intended dance here was not to take place, so now we are alone again though we had a large party at luncheon, the four New Englanders whom we saw on the course yesterday, Mr Grey and Mr Massey. It is unfortunate the New England party should have chosen these races for their visit; they were so bad and the Lake so dull: my aunt being ill, and my uncle worried about business matters, prevented any extra gaiety here. Of course we did not care about the dance, but a visit to the Lake or a party here is always looked forward to with pleasure by our friends. Mr M'Donald, the C.C.L., New England, is a very clever man. Unfortunately he is very short with a small hump on his back just at the waist. It was owing to this peculiarity that he at one time possessed so much influence over the natives about here. They had some time previously a very favourite and powerful chief who had the same deformity, and they, according to their established superstition, imagined that at his death he had "jumped up" or arisen again a white man. Mr M'Donald encouraged them in this belief and added to his popularity with them by studying their language and customs. Mr Bligh is just a youth, clerk of Petty Sessions under Mr M'Donald. Mr Elliot was formerly A.D.C. to Sir Charles Gipps, good-looking and agreeable. Next comes Mr Goldfinch, goldenhaired, whiskered, and eyebrowed, I thought it was a nickname, and Mr Derby the hero of yesterday's hurdle race. After lunch we had some music and then put on our habits, intending to show our new acquaintances the delights of the beach and the beauties of Tacking Point, but found it was too late for them to return to the Settlement by that route, so we accompanied them as far as Halcyon Place, where we said goodbye, hoping for a merrier meeting at some future time. Mr Maister has been here for a day, and Mr Marlow, the latter lost his horse at Tod's which delayed him. Mr Tod himself we have not seen but we hear he brought letters to Annie Jobling telling of the birth of her nephew.

On Monday, 5th July 1847, our nice Highland maid, Christina Ross, was married to Mr Michael Fahye. Mr Purvis performed the ceremony in the drawing-room, where Bruce and Helen were married just three years ago. Christina has been with us ever since she arrived in the Colony, nine and a half years ago; we shall miss her dreadfully. I had said long ago that when she married I would be her bridesmaid, so when the day was fixed she reminded me of this, and I said if my aunt did not object I would be most happy to keep my promise. So I drew off her gloves and cut the cake—the two great duties of a bridesmaid. The bride, who is tall, fair and handsome, looked very well in her dress of white muslin, with a handsome worked cape. She wore a cap trimmed with white satin ribbon, a white satin sash and bows. After the ceremony we all went to the dining-room, where we drank the health of the bride and bridegroom, and wished them happiness. Strange to say, I had never seen the latter till yesterday, though he has been an admirer of Christina for some time. He is tall and dark and young. His father was a soldier, who got a small grant of land from the Government, and settled at Roland Plains, where he has a good house and farm, to which they went at once. I do hope she will be happy. I wish mamma had been here.

12th July. I am dreadfully tired tonight. We have had some very fatiguing reels. If Baron Munchausen's dog ran his leg off, I have nearly danced my feet off, and all in the vain hope of thereby curing my chilblains. I have also been working very hard in my garden. I have dug up all my ground-nuts, and am much disappointed at the smallness of the crop. Mr Woodward called, and is in high indignation with the Bishop (Broughton), who lately refused to confirm some young ladies at Bathurst, because they had been seen in a Presbyterian church—a crime, in the opinion of such a High Church man, or Puseyite, as he must be.

My uncle has returned from Yarrows. It really is wonderful the amount of work he gets through, mentally and bodily. It is most trying to think that much of this has been thrown away through what appears to be the wrong-headedness of some people who ought to have known better.

15th July. We have had letters from dear mamma. She is going to Bathurst this week to see Aunt Annabella and her family, who are all there on their way from Glen Logan to St Clair (near Singleton) where they are now going to live. I wish they had come to Sydney before we left Sydney.

Wednesday, 28th July 1847, Margaret's eighteenth birthday. I have just been writing to Maria Grey, whose birthday it also is, to wish her many happy returns. They still argue as to which is the elder. I say certainly Margaret, as Maria was born in Edinburgh. Yesterday we were all invited by "Sir Gustavus and Lady Gordina Innes" to an entertainment at their Bower. It was quite a gay scene, with flags flying, and festoons of shells and flowers. The guests behaved with the greatest propriety, but I heard afterwards that one of them carried off the dinner table, a novel way of shewing appreciation of the feast.

I have lately been reading a charming book, Steven's *Central America,* about the wonderful antiquities of that country. I could scarcely tear myself away from the contemplation of some of the curious sketches of carved stone pillars and what appears to be altars. I have copied a few of them. There is a book here just now I am very anxious to read—*Glimpses of the Old World,* by an American. It, of course, is very different, as history throws light on much of it. I have learned from it the names of the Seven Hills of Rome, and how I may remember them by a word made from the initial letters VE—Q—CAP—C, which stand for Venicual, Equaline, Querinale, Celian, Aventine, Palatine, Capitoliux.[1]

On 6th August my uncle and Gustavus left in the steamer for Sydney. We shall miss the dear boy very much. He is now at school at Stroud, and quite happy with nice boys of his own age. Gordy and he gave a farewell tea at Banqueting Hall, a charming spot, from which there is a lovely view of lake and sea, and Mr Mackay has gone to Sydney to see some horses shipped for India, among them Willesby Rockey and Sir Bertram, the last a beautiful creature. I have been busy knitting edging and am now working a collar for Aunt Barbara, and as usual making many plans for drawing and working. I am too apt to procrastinate, and forget the good maxim—

> Time was, time is, and time will cease to be—
> Time present is the only time for me.

31st August. Mr Smith has been reading aloud to us every evening from after tea till ten o'clock, and has finished *Martin Chuzzlewit.* It is just the book for reading aloud, and he reads very well. I think even the author would say he had done it justice. We have had some fun appropriating characters from it. Margaret is Mercy, I am Charity, Dido is Miss Todgers, and patronizes Mr Smith, who is pronounced by all to be her "youngest young man" (no doubt).

Saturday night, 11th September 1847. It seems like a month since last Saturday. On Friday forenoon, the 3rd, Mr Purvis

---

[1] Viminalis, Esquilinus, Quirinalis, Caelius, Aventinus, Palatinus, Capitolinus.

WHEN THE GOVERNOR CAME (1847)

came out and told my aunt of her mother's death, which took place at Tivoli on 13th August, exactly three weeks before. It was indeed a sad shock to her, as she had no idea that Mrs Macleay was seriously ill. The last letters, dated 12th, merely mentioned that she was not very well, so nothing fatal was apprehended. Mr Purvis also said that when he left the Manning my uncle was daily expected there, which kept us very anxious expecting him here any moment. On Saturday night my aunt was very unwell, and I think the past week will long be remembered by us as one of the most unhappy times of our lives.

On Sunday 12th my aunt was better, and we had the morning service in the schoolroom as usual. Then as her feet were very cold we persuaded her to have a hot bottle for them, and to take a rest on her sofa in her dressing-room. In a few minutes we heard her calling for Dido, and on running down found that the cork had flown out of the bottle and the hot water run out over her feet. We got flour immediately and covered them from the air, and this proved a wonderful remedy. In the midst of our anxieties a steamer appeared in sight, and never did we greet one with greater satisfaction. The wind was fair, the day was fine, but alas the tiresome bar was too rough for her to get in, as we heard her waiting till seven o'clock.

Next morning Mr Smith went to the Settlement before breakfast. The bar was if anything worse, the same report again in the evening. On Tuesday morning, we heard that a boat with great difficulty got within speaking distance of the steamer. My uncle was on board, but Captain Parsons had decided to run up to Trial Bay as they were short of water. This was indeed a dismal prospect, but at eleven o'clock, to our surprise and joy, my uncle arrived. He had landed in one of the steamer's boats, which really was dangerous in the state of the weather. That evening the steamer got in, but stayed only one day, and was off again on Thursday morning, taking my uncle with her. His visit seems like a dream, a pleasant one indeed, as it has left my aunt much better. We had letters from dear mamma, who had just returned to Sydney, but not in time to come by the steamer, which was fortunate.

Thursday, 16th September 1847. And now begins a new era in my existence. I am no longer an infant, but a full-grown child, arrived at the so-called years of discretion. My aunt kindly said we might have luncheon at the beach, or do anything we liked better; so with one consent, we spent the morning working in our garden, and after luncheon rode to the sandy flat near the Settlement. Mr Salway went on to ask if a steamer passing had left a mail. It had not, and Mr Smith helped us to gather some wild flowers, which I have been drawing. An amusing poem has come to hand, the subject, "The Port Macquarie Races", telling how four happy young squatters set out, accompanied by two flunkeys, on donkeys. Two black boys, as pack boys, and a fat individual, came from Dundee.

> So hurrah for the road, and although we're now sorry,
> We'll banish all care when we reach Port Macquarie.

Monday, 4th October. There is a most violent storm raging outside. We have been very anxious about the *Mary Ann*, which left Port Macquarie on Thursday, taking with her twenty passengers, and having accommodation only for six. Mr Smith left in her; he has been here more than three months. He has just heard of his father's death. We are very sorry for him, so far away from his home and all his own people. He is only twenty, and does not like this country, especially the bush.

I may here add that we never saw poor Mr Smith again, and to this day I sometimes wonder who he was, and what became of him. He got safely to Sydney, and there reported himself to the gentleman who introduced him to my uncle, and who did so in the hope that employment might be found for him on one of his out-stations. This was tried, but failed. A place was now found for him in an office in Sydney. He then went to Melbourne, but returned to Sydney. The day he arrived there he called on the lady with whom he had previously boarded, and asked her if she could give him a room as before. It was then arranged that he should bring his luggage, etc., from the steamer that night or next morning. He never returned, and from that hour no one has seen or heard of him. Every inquiry was made at the time. He never went back to the steamer for his luggage; if any inquiries or letters ever came from England we were not told; in fact we knew nothing whatever of his people, not even their name, which I am pretty sure was not Smith. Once he said to me in deep indignation, "I cannot stand young B———. He despises me because I cannot rub down and saddle my horse. He knows nothing of books, and the work in which I have spent my life. Mathematics and languages mean nothing to him; he is as ignorant as my father's grooms." I believe he had been at Addiscombe and expected to go to India, but why he was banished from his home and prospects I cannot even guess. He was a gentlemanlike youth, and my uncle, I know, was anxious to be of use to him.

16th October. Got up very early and churned, which means also that I skimmed the milk, and made up the butter. Lately I have taken charge of the dairy and like it very much. It began to rain this evening, real steady rain, the first we have had since February, eight whole months, quite unusual in this district; but alas for my castle building, the next day was as fine as possible and the rain had not sunk into the earth one inch.

Friday, 22nd October. Here I am once more established in my own snug little room, with everything so neat and comfortable, and the cause of my being here again is so delightful, dear mamma has returned after being away six months and a half—how glad and thankful [*sic*] we are to see her again. Saturday and Sunday it rained steadily, which will be good for everything but the hay, which they began to cut yesterday. I got up early to plant seed in my garden.

Wednesday, 27th October. Mr Salway left yesterday for the Macleay. We have returned with great zeal to our burning off; it really is most laborious work. I can do little but sleep or eat afterwards which shows it agrees with me. Mamma is looking so much better than when she went to Sydney. She was at a Jewish marriage while there, and has described the ceremony to us. It is true that there is a glass handed round, the contents of which the bridal party drink, the bridegroom then throws it on the floor and stamps on it, thereby signifying that when the broken glass reunites the parties then joined shall separate. The service was partly in English, and partly in Hebrew, and in substance much like that in our own prayerbook.

30th October. Mr Charles Grey came out to call yesterday, and was amazed to find we had not breakfasted! He stayed till four o'clock. Mr Marlow came out to say goodbye: he is going to Sydney and from there to New Zealand. We shall remember him by his amusing song, "The King of Otakiti". Mr Mackay is still here.

Thursday, 4th November. Our burning off has been put an end to by a very tragic event, a branch of a large tree falling on poor Eliza. She had just trotted up the hill with her pretty little foal, when a great branch from a half burnt tree fell on her and broke her back. We were all at the lake at the time, and though we regret Eliza's fate very much (she was the prettiest of our cream-coloured ponies) we are very thankful we were not on the hill at the time.

12th November. We have all had influenza, and hear it has been very bad in Melbourne and Sydney. We were very sorry to have the report of Rodrick M'Leod's death confirmed. It said in the paper, "From want of medical advice", which seems odd if they are still at Geelong, as there must be doctors there as it is now a populous place. We heard afterwards that he was at an out-station far from any doctor.

29th November. Nothing particular has happened of late, except that we have all had influenza. My uncle is still away, and my aunt speaks of spending Christmas in Sydney, which I hope they may all do, otherwise they will not see the Dumaresq boys who go to England in the *Agincourt*. Mrs Onslow, too, will not be remaining much longer in this country, and she is taking her eldest daughter, Georgy, away with her.

The weather has been very stormy, but we have had two short rides, as Dr Fattorini, who has been here several times lately, recommends it. My aunt has had influenza very badly. All the Tisdale family have it now. The baby, of which they are very proud, was christened last Sunday "Eliza", after Dido. So impressed was Mrs Payne (the godmother) with the honour, that on being asked by the clergyman to name the child she said "Miss Eliza", not liking I suppose to be too familiar. It reminded me of the story of a good woman who on a similar occasion answered "Lucy, Sir." "Lucifer!" exclaimed the clergyman, indignantly; "Not at all. I will give the child a good Christian name"—and promptly christened the little girl George Washington.

I continue to teach the children, who come now to the Servants' Hall, which is more convenient than the veranda. We were much amused lately by the Churchill children. Dido was teaching Sarah to read the sentence, "Ann is a good girl," which she told her to spell "A double n" and "g double o d", but Sarah would say always "A n n". So Dido turned to her brother, and said—"I am sure you know, Henry, what you should say when you see two n's together?" "Please ma'am," said the delighted Henry, "I would say there's two pullets."

6th December. My uncle has written to say he will bring Gustavus home with him by the next trip of the *Phoenix,* the Clarence River steamer, which now lands passengers at Port Macquarie. This puts an end to the expectation of going to Sydney at present.

Friday, 10th December. Poor Gordy, who we thought had quite recovered, has had a relapse. Dr Fattorini stayed all night, and says he finds the lake air agrees so well with him he will come out to stop every other night. Poor man, he has suffered so much pain that any relief from it is eagerly seized.

I must say he is very clever, and agreeable. He brought out his two youngest children one afternoon—Clemence and Eugene. They are very nice-looking. The latter is my aunt's god-son.

14th December. Mr Patrick M'Kay has returned from New England, and tells us Mr Taylor has been thrown from his horse and broken his leg badly. The family had just arrived safely at their station.

Friday, 17th December 1847. Dr Fattorini called, looking wretchedly ill. He told us that a report had reached Port Macquarie (from the Manning) that the Governor's carriage had been upset, and Lady Mary thrown out and killed on the spot; but this is too shocking a tale to be believed on so slight a foundation. Reports of this kind are almost always exaggerated. Teasdale killed a death adder today on the hill. It really was quite pretty, of a yellowish-brown colour, spotted, and not more than fourteen inches long. The prettiest snake I have ever seen was one that came from under the nursery veranda. It was slate colour, and very long and thin. Old George fired a gun at it. When it heard the report it raised its head about two feet from the ground for a moment, then quickly disappeared.

Monday, 20th December. Mamma and my cousins walked to the beach and brought back some beautiful pieces of seaweed. We have now a good many varieties dried and fastened neatly into a book. They look so pretty. It quite repays one for the trouble of arranging them.

We expected my uncle and Gustavus on Thursday, and the carriage was sent to Port Macquarie for them, but the bar was so rough that a boat could not go out for them, so they went on to the Clarence in the steamer, and did not arrive till the following Thursday, and narrowly escaped having to return to Sydney.

Much to our regret my uncle has confirmed the report of the awfully sudden death of poor Lady Mary Fitzroy. The family had all been staying at Government House, Parramatta, and were going to Sydney to spend Christmas. About ten o'clock on the morning of the 9th, Lady Mary entered the carriage, a heavy travelling chariot. It had been some time at the door and the horses were restless. Sir Charles, who was to drive, was seated on the box with Mr Chester Master, his A.D.C., beside him. A servant sat behind. Scarcely had the grooms released their hold upon the horses, when the leaders made a bound forward and set off at full speed down the hill to the entrance gate. Had the road been straight possibly the accident might not have happened, but unhappily at the gate there is a sharp turning, and there the carriage which had been swaying from side to side all the way down the hill upset heavily, throwing all in it out with great violence. Mr Fitzroy who had watched them from the house rushed down followed by all who were near, but alas before he arrived life had fled, and the fond mother who had but a few short minutes before gaily bade him goodbye, now lay a bleeding and mangled corpse, blood flowing from her mouth and ears, and her chest crushed in by part of the carriage which had fallen upon her. Who can describe the horror of such a moment? Sir Charles, whose fall had been broken by his having kept hold of the reins, although much hurt managed to reach the spot, and there gazed on her in speechless agony.[1] Poor Mr Master lay at a short distance crushed insensible and bleeding, but life was not yet extinct. Several doctors were immediately on the spot, but nothing could be done for him and he died the same evening without regaining even momentary consciousness. The footman was but slightly hurt.

This dreadful event has caused universal sorrow throughout the Colony. Lady Mary had travelled so much in the country and become personally acquainted with so many of its inhabitants that they feel as if a dear friend had been snatched away from them. All who had seen her, and all who had heard of her, unite in bewailing her sudden and melancholy end, not that they sorrow as those without hope, for no one but a true Christian could have possessed the many virtues of this most kind and excellent lady. This most sad accident occurred

[1] A monument in Parramatta Park marks the spot.

WHEN THE GOVERNOR CAME (1847)

on Tuesday, 7th December. The funeral took place on the 10th, when the remains of Lady Mary Fitzroy and Lieut. C. Chester Master were deposited in the same vault in the Parramatta burying ground, attended by an immense concourse of people, whose grief was best expressed by their silent and orderly conduct. My uncle, who was present, describes the scene as most affecting, and so far on this sad occasion had self been forgotten by all, that the people who came from a distance were unable to get anything to eat, the shopkeepers, instead of profiting by such an unusual concourse of people coming to their town, had neglected to make any preparations for them. The bakers had no bread, the hotelkeepers no supplies, and every shop was shut, and people talked together in whispers. My uncle went to see the Governor; he is in the deepest affliction. He said, "It is only one short week since I handed her into the carriage to go to a wedding," (Miss Macarthur to Mr George Lesley) and they were then hastening to Sydney to be present at the wedding of Miss Baldock to Mr Carlo O'Connel. Poor Miss Baldock, hers has been a sad, sad bridal. In the beginning of the year her marriage was put off owing to the loss of her sister and brother-in-law in the wreck of the *Sovereign*, and now it has taken place on the day of Lady Mary's funeral.

Chapter

9

FAREWELL
TO THE LAKE

T HE YEAR CLOSED rather sadly: we spent a very quiet Christmas, and had no house party. On the 31st Colonel Grey
brought Maria to spend a week with us, he had returned some
time before, finding the new settlements quite unsuitable for
his family. On New Year's day the usual guests rode out to
dinner. The kindly welcome was unchanged, but we all felt that
"bad times" meant something we had never before realized—
in as far as they had brought cares and anxieties to our elders
—and other troubles might follow.

It had before this been definitely arranged that my uncle,
aunt, and cousins were all to go to Sydney for three months,
leaving mamma, Margaret, and me in possession, with occa-
sional visits from Mr Patrick Mackay during their absence.
Meantime we were busy helping in their preparation, and Gordy
took me to her peahen's nest, which she had lately found with
five eggs in it, and gave me many instructions about managing
it. The pea-fowls, dear delightful creatures, are to be my especial
charge, and Margaret is to take charge of the parrot.

Dido and I had letters from Aunt Jane Innes, who always
writes to us both on the same day, addressing one as Miss
Innes of Lake Innes, the other, Miss Innes at Lake Innes—she

tells us of Mr and Mrs Benjamin Wemyss, and their son and heir, and she also mentions Mr Gunn as still in search of a situation—poor "Pine", he is always on the same errand.

10th January 1848. We were all up at dawn, which, after all was wiser than our former plan of sitting up all night so as to be up in good time in the morning—I said goodbye to Mr Salway and Captain Parsons who left about five o'clock. Mr Hugh also left before breakfast. At eight my uncle, aunt, and cousins took their departure leaving us disconsolate. We have made many resolutions to be very industrious during their absence, and after taking a farewell look at the steamer from the flagstaff, we sat down to work at the patchwork tablecover, which, though it is not unpicked every night like Penelope's web, seems likely to be as long in hand. We went out to gather some fruit and found the trees covered with parrots. There was little to be got after them, as when once they have tasted it they will not consent to be driven away.

13th January. Rain! Rain!! Rain!!! Delicious, for it does not keep one in the house. I have been working hard in my garden, and then had a delightful bath, but oh! so cold. In the evening we had a dreadful fright—George and the cook being rather excited, the former locked the back door at eight o'clock, and much to our relief, took his departure. Presently we heard voices in the back yard—and someone attempting to open the back door. Mamma went to the office window, and said there was a strange man in the back veranda. This did not tend to reassure us as the noise at the back door continued. She at last went to ask who was there, and found that old George had just arrived on the scene with the key of the back door, and was trying to open it for Mr Mackay, who was quite wet through, having ridden the whole way from the Macleay, about seventy miles, in the pouring rain. We were delighted to see him, as we feared the rivers would rise and prevent him returning, which they would have done had he waited another day. And now, what could we give him to eat? The cook had forgotten to bake,

*"No pen or pencil could
do justice to this perfect day."*

FAREWELL TO THE LAKE

but was so civil, and wished to do anything and everything—but did nothing. George threw down the pantry key declaring he would away to his bed, and we might manage things as we liked, which was just what we could not do; but at last some food was got, and we retired to bed, well pleased to have the young gentleman safely back to look after the household, our short experience of George and the cook not being satisfactory.

14th January. Got up very early, gathered up all the fallen apples, and picked all the ripe raspberries, then went to visit the peahen, and to my horror found her standing up in her nest, while a perfect stream of water flowed over the five precious eggs. I flew to mamma to ask her what I should do, and she advised me to remove them at once, which I did, carrying Mrs Pea with me, but she refused to sit in the nest we had prepared for her, so we got a hen who seemed quite delighted to take her place, much to our relief: all this time it continued to pour, and so on for the rest of the day.

17th January. The lake has risen to a great size, covering whole banks of reeds which have encroached on it. We are afraid it will break through again at Cati Creek. Picked some raspberries which continue to ripen in spite of the rain.

Saturday, 22nd January. No pen or pencil could do justice to the beauty of this perfect day. It was clear, cloudless, lovely, and we enjoyed it all the more as we had not seen much of the sun for nearly a fortnight.

5th February. I wrote such long letters to my cousins that my journal has of late been quite neglected. We had a great disappointment this morning when the last [*sic*] returned from Port M'Quarie and we heard a passing steamer had not called, and that the *Mary Ann,* which the cook announces daily he has seen from the hills, has not yet arrived. Great was our surprise when later in the day we received a large packet of letters, "Favoured by Mr Hugh Mackay" who we supposed was at Moreton Bay! He had come overland from Raymond Terrace.

On Sunday all the children appeared at afternoon service—and I heard them their hymns and Catechism. The Churchills made most startling remarks. Today I was shewing them a picture of David and Goliath, when Henry burst forth into the history of "Jack the Giant Killer", whose exploits he related with great glee. My children, Teasdales, are slower in expressing their ideas.

7th February. Mamma has had the grapes picked to make wine, but the birds have been so destructive she fears there will not be much. I picked some fresh apples for a squab pie, and prepared some grapes for jam, which occupied me till lunch was ready. Afterwards finding that the cook was out, I carried my materials to the marble slab, and determined to make the pie myself—but before I tell what this famous squab pie was composed of I shall give my opinion of its merits by saying that though it is possible I may make another, it is highly improbable I shall taste it. Mr Hugh was of a different opinion, or pretended to be, for he dined on it—and insisted on doing so. The pie is made of layers of apples and beef steak covered with pie crust, and baked, pepper and salt of course, but cook says I should have added an onion.

9th February. We all went to the stables with Mr H. Mackay to see his new horses—Musselman, Colonel, and Gustavus, and a mule Jacko, which he got from Captain Parsons. Rode to Cati, the beach apparently good, but full of soft patches which we call quicksands, of which I have the greatest horror; saw an empty barrel, several trees, and a log of cedar, which have been washed ashore during the late storms. I rode Chimpanzie, a creature that I hate.

11th February. The steamer is still detained in Port M'Quarie: the bar is so rough, and only eight feet of water on it—the steamer requires ten and a half.

Valentine's Day. But not a valentine appeared at the Lake. However, we need not despair, as last year mine did not arrive till April. We all rode to Blackman's Point and found Miss

FAREWELL TO THE LAKE

Jobling alone—she leads a most solitary life. I rode Dandy, and mamma had Bolter—our own horses being still absent without leave. I must say that however superior my neighbour's horses may be, I much prefer my own.

15th February. We had a very early breakfast as the gentlemen wished to start immediately on their long journey, but it was three o'clock before they set off, leaving us quite disconsolate— "Who will fill their vacant places, who will sing their songs tonight?" We went to the gate for a parting look. Mr Patrick led Imperial, with a great pack on its back—it looked like an elephant with a howdah. Mr Hugh rode Gustavus. I do not envy him his long journey which he expects will take at least a fortnight.

Friday, 18th February. There was no dew last night, which is quite unusual when the weather is fine. The great event of the day was that the gardener when mowing the lawn found the peahen sitting on five eggs. Her nest is sheltered by a branch of the Norfolk Island pine-trees. We are surprised at her laying again so soon. The pea-chicks are not yet five weeks old—they are lovely little things, and so strong—they fly both far and high, and roost in a tree at night which their good foster mother does not approve of—she took to the eggs most kindly, and the whole five came out. Now they are just beginning to shew their crests. We have just heard that the *Mary Ann* has been obliged to run to Trial Bay, the wind is so strong and the sea so rough. The cook, who is too often in a state of oblivion, has crushed two of his fingers in attempting to put a large log of wood in the kitchen fire. He insists in keeping on a huge fire as if he was preparing to roast at least a baron of beef.

20th February. A lovely day with a north wind, the first we have had for weeks. Gathered some figs, which are just now both good and plentiful. There is a beautiful pink and white lily in flower in the garden, the first we have seen.

21st February. Where do you suppose I went first this morning? To the stable yard, but only to look at my friends there—

yesterday I was more active. Shankland (the groom) being away, and the cook gone to visit the Churchills, I thought the poor horses would fare badly, so went to see after them, and found that they had not had anything to eat. I got them some of the grass the gardener had just mowed, which they quite enjoyed. Fortunately there was only one horse, and Mr Hugh's mule—anyone would have laughed at my endeavours to feed them, but not a soul was near. I could not help thinking of the great change a few months had brought. We then thought it quite an event to visit the stables, and always with my uncle, and we never ventured near the large entrance gates, but now I went in and out, looked at the new stables, and got some corn from the old. The busy scene was quite deserted, and no one knew I had been there. Mr Patrick Mackay, to our surprise, arrived about sunset, having seen his brother well started. He brought me a letter from Maria Grey, who tells me that her little brother, whom she began to teach only a month ago, is already in words of three letters. Margaret, who has not been very well, has had a visit from Dr M'Intyre, who has forbidden her to take milk in any shape. He says it does not agree with everyone in this climate, and of late we have used it freely—in butter, cream, curds, etc. She had a most painful rash on her right shoulder, which spread round half her body.

Friday, 3rd March 1848. Dear Gordy's birthday. She today enters her teens. We spent a very quiet day: very different from this day last year when the Governor and party arrived. My cousins mention having seen him in Sydney, and that he was looking very sad.

4th March. Mr Massie called and remained for some time, making himself very agreeable. He amused us very much, explaining the performance of Punch and Judy. I wonder it has not yet been introduced in Sydney. He then told us of his visit to Captain Jobling the last time he was down staying with Mr Gray. It had been raining for some days. At last a bright morning dawned to the joy of everyone, especially the teller of

FAREWELL TO THE LAKE

the tale, who proposed to Mr Gray and Mr Salway that they should all go and dine at Gooloowa. N.B.—It does not appear that they were invited or expected—but they all agreed to go, and that it would be most agreeable to go all the way by boat, so they got some black boys who pulled them up the river—this they found very delightful. They were well received by Captain Jobling, and had a very good dinner, but alas! before they had quite finished, the clouds which had been gathering suddenly broke, and rain fell in torrents. Mr Massie rose and joined Miss Jobling in the drawing-room, then seeing no prospect of the weather clearing, returned to the dining-room to hint that it was time to go. Mr Gray rose in a bearish humour, not liking to be disturbed over his wine, and as no one asked them to remain they walked down to the wharf. Their boat was gone: they called, they stamped, they cooe'd—but no one answered. At last the punt came from Blackman's Point, and they crossed to the other side. Of course, there were no horses for them there, as they had come from the settlement in a boat. There was nothing for it but a walk of four miles on a road they had in the morning pronounced unfit to ride on—and where they now had to wade in muddy water sometimes over their ankles—and, sighed poor Mr Massie, "I had on a pair of smart new boots, and my trousers strapped down." Fortunately Mr Salway had provided himself with a mackintosh, and Mr Gray, indignant with the proposer of this expedition, marched on in silence. It turned out that the blacks had taken the boat to a sheltered place, where they secured it, and then crept into a hollow log for further shelter for themselves, not thinking that their services would be required while the rain continued.

5th March. Poured without intermission all day. In the evening received letters by the *Mary Ann* which set at rest our anxieties as to the arrival or non-arrival of the steamer. Our party are still all at Brownlow Hill. For the next five days the rain continued more or less heavily—everything in the house feels damp—and a smell of paint pervades the whole place. Out of doors the birds have eaten up all the peaches, and have

Farewell to the Lake

now attacked the few figs left by the rain. The furcroyas are growing so tremendously, that if they do not flower soon, they will be like Jack's bean stalk, and grow up out of sight. The cook has been behaving very badly. The other day he went out after putting the bread into the oven, which had not been properly heated, and there he left it until it was too hard and dried up to be used; where the people get the spirits is more than we can imagine, but one or all of them are continually more than half intoxicated.

Friday, 10th March. We were on the qui vive the whole morning, each sound we heard we thought might be the carriage arriving. The steamer had been distinctly seen rounding Tacking Point, and while we wondered at the delay each gave a finishing touch in their own especial department—and when all was in readiness we found that the steamer had existed only in the imagination of those who said they saw it—a sort of flying Dutchman that takes various shapes according to what they are expecting. At night we had a terrific thunderstorm, wind and rain in equal violence. It poured without ceasing for hours, and the thunder and lightning were dreadful. None of us could sleep, and at last mamma and Margaret came to my room to get a candle lighted as their matches were damp— we found that one of the schoolroom windows had been left open and the wind having changed the rain was blown in. This was the first flood—but every bedroom was inundated through their fireplaces, and we wandered about like ghosts, with basins and house-cloths in our hands drying up the water as it came in, till about four o'clock, when the storm abated.

23rd March. This is the third Thursday we have retired to rest hoping that the next morning we should welcome home my aunt and cousins—may the third bring its reputed good fortune. On Wednesday 15th the Maitland passed here, but could not get into port till the following Monday owing to the bar—she left again yesterday, taking with her all Dr Fattorini's family. The *Mary Ann,* which left two days earlier, took twenty-one passengers, only five of them intending to return to the district. Alas! Poor Port M'Quarie! It is indeed a deserted village. As this was the last trip of the *Maitland* it makes the time of the return of the family more uncertain than ever, as now they can only come in a steamer that will stop and land them (it actually was the 27th April before they arrived).

29th March. We walked to the poultry yard and found that the native dogs had been very troublesome and had carried off four ducks and some fowls. Thomas, the old sailor, shewed us some tiny ducklings.

31st March. Made two pineapples into jelly—when peeled they weighed 3½ lbs. each. The gardener weighed several lately, the heaviest weighing 4 lbs. 1 oz. They are very fine and plentiful but none of us like them. I made the jelly as we do apples, but it never jellied properly, and is more like honey both in colour and substance. In the evening had a delightful ride. We have been busy tidying up Lantana Bower, but so many young plants have sprung up they quite spoil the place, and are likely to become a nuisance.

1st April. Forgot the date, and so fell a victim to a wicked plot! Christina came out to see us and stayed till Monday, which was fortunate for us as the horrid cook had gone off after setting bread and never came back to bake it. So she helped us, and fried some chops while I laid the table for dinner. After waiting in vain for George, we found he had gone to bed! It really is too provoking, they just do as they please, knowing the difficulty there would be in getting others to fill their places if they were sent away.

2nd April. Dido's 16th birthday. Churchill has brought us some sweet potatoes, the first I have ever seen. They are large and of a round shape, which he says is because he has left them in the ground since last season, and that generally they are smaller, and more oval.

Monday, 10th April. I have a tragic tale to tell of the pea-chicks and the good black hen, their foster mother, who disappeared during the night. We heard the peacock making a noise, and supposed something had disturbed him, but thought the young birds would be quite safe, as they roosted on a tree quite near the nursery veranda, but a native dog must have attacked them. Some of the feathers of the hen were found near the front gate, but no trace of the pea-fowls. Those that are left are wandering about miserably in search of their lost friends. Mr and Mrs Purvis called, bringing their two fine little boys.

11th April. We drove to Port M'Quarie, where mamma wished to see after her goods and chattels, and to make some calls. We waited in Mrs Gloag's room while she went to see poor Christina whose little baby has died. We called on Mrs Paterson, and saw all the family, a large party of little creatures. Helen was at home, and shewed us some of her drawings. From Mrs Purvis we heard of Mr Wilson, the artist, who has been growing raisin grapes and figs at the Macleay, but unsuccessfully, in preference to following his profession. He has now decided on establishing himself in Sydney. Mr Purvis has had his likeness taken, and took us to see it. The style is coloured chalks, not quite life size, and we thought it good. Mr Wilson shewed us a bird he had got at the Macleay and thinks it is the first of the kind that has been shot, as they are very rare and shy. He intends to send this specimen home to Mr Gould, the famous ornithologist. It is of a brownish colour, with green and bronze feathers on its back and neck, has long legs, and a very long bill rather hooked. I could not examine it as closely as I would have liked to do. Mamma called on Mrs Scott who has taken a house for a month for change and sea bathing. A large bunch of bananas has been brought in. We have also picked some ripe loquats.

Friday, 21st April. Disappointed again, but again is the hope renewed that we shall see them all tomorrow. There was some rain in the morning and a beautiful rainbow. Had the tale been true that there is a pot of gold at each end of a rainbow, we might have made our fortunes, as both ends were within the

"We drove to Port M'Quarie."

grounds round the house. It has just struck me that in one sense it may be true, and possibly gave rise to the saying, for the rain that accompanies the rainbow causes the earth to produce what is worth many pots of gold. We have received a newspaper in which there is a letter from someone at Wellington describing the effects of a bite from a death adder, and mentioning poor Mrs Morrissy, whose death we had already heard of. She was servant once at the White Rock, a soldier's wife, and very superior woman. She survived only three hours after she was bitten. She was walking, after dark, from the house to the kitchen, when at the door of the latter she trod on something which, from the sound it made they thought was a cat; but she insisted that it was a snake, and on searching carefully, they found that she was only too right. It is supposed that the sting is in the tail. The wound it made was very small, just below the ankle bone; it was sucked immediately, and a piece cut out. She was kept moving about till, feeling a numbness in her limbs and excessive fatigue, she begged to be allowed to rest. Her

FAREWELL TO THE LAKE

eyelids became quite paralysed, and in three hours after the bite she expired so gently and without pain so that those around her could scarcely tell when she ceased to breathe. She from the first thought she could not recover.

Sunday, 23rd April. We got a letter from Mr Gloag telling us that the steamer had passed in the morning, taking Major Innes and his family on to the Clarence River. This was a blow, but we consoled ourselves with the hope that in a few days they would all be with us.

24th April. Christina and her husband came out to see us. His farming has been a failure, and he has taken a place as storekeeper at Innes Creek.

Thursday, 27th April. We all rose very early so as to be in readiness to receive our travellers, but were still in our dressing gowns when George announced that the carriage was in sight, and before we could go to receive them my aunt and cousins were in the house, and after all our preparations we were taken completely by surprise. My aunt is well, but thin; Dido is stouter. Mr Onslow only has come with them, as he intends to return overland. They did not dislike their voyage to the Clarence, where they were well entertained at the Grafton Hotel.

May Day. The grey dawn was breaking when we got up, and, of course, we all washed our faces in the "magical May dew". Already we have forgotten the last four months, and everything seems quite as usual. We have had some delightful rides, and after dinner, music—Margaret and I sang a duet. My cousins saw the Misses Gore at Tivoli, and are charmed with them and their singing. I wish I could hear Miss Isobell; everyone says she sings exquisitely. We have received a parcel containing two handsome knitted shawls, afterwards came a letter from Christina saying they were from her—it is really too kind and generous of her.

Thursday, 4th May. We all rose very early to see Mr Onslow who started for Sydney overland. He had promised to return and bring his family here at the end of the month, if he can get a steamer to call at Port M'Quarie with them. My uncle thinks this can be arranged, and if they come Miss Macleay will come with them.

I may here say that Mr Onslow did not succeed in getting a steamer going north to call and land passengers at Port M'Quarie, as it involved also calling for them. So they all went back to India without our seeing any of them again.

Not long after my uncle and aunt returned from Sydney the cook gave notice that he wished to leave. This was most unexpected and annoying, as he was a most capable man, and a good cook, though of late his conduct had not been altogether satisfactory. Edwards, the gardener, had already left, and now comes the reason of their departure, and an explanation of their extraordinary conduct during my aunt's absence and at other times previously. In the wine cellar was a large cask of port wine—a pipe I believe it was called. It had stood there for some time, and arrangements were now being made for having the wine bottled and laid carefully away. There was some unexplained delay in preparing the bottles. At last all was in readiness. The cask had been tapped some months previously, but when the brass tap was turned it did not act. A new air hole was made in the top of the cask, but still no wine flowed out.

Then a long reed was got, and lowered down from the new spigot; it shewed that the cask was empty all but about twelve inches, the height at which the brass cock had been inserted. It was quite impossible that the cask had leaked. The question was—what then had become of the wine? Naturally my uncle was very much annoyed. All sorts of conjectures were started. My aunt had always kept the key of the cellar herself locked safely in a drawer in her storeroom. During her absence the key was left in Mr Patrick Mackay's, who had opened the door only once, just to see that all was right, which apparently it was. No solution of the mystery had occurred to anyone, when old George said "he wondered that no one had ever considered that there might be a way from the kitchen to the cellar, it being directly below".

On close examination this was found to be the case. The wicked cook, trusted and well treated, had, with the aid of the gardener, been carrying on a system of robbery for months—possibly years. They had cut a small trapdoor in the wooden floor of the kitchen in a corner, which being quite unsuspected was easily concealed. They had been equally clever in hiding their place of entrance to the cellar which was large and rather dark, and well filled with cases of various sizes—many of these cases were found to be entirely empty or to contain only empty bottles and straw. I do not think George had assisted the other two, but he must have had strong suspicions of their doings and partaken often of the stolen wine, with which they no no doubt plied him when they intended to visit the cellar. It was thought that the cook disposed of the wine in the settlement or had a depôt somewhere; he had opportunities of taking it when he went in his cart for wood. He had a horse and cart for his own use, and was always very obliging in going messages to Port M'Quarie, and bringing in wood.

Some quiet months followed. My uncle was often away. Port M'Quarie was almost deserted. Gustavus was at school, and our friends the Messrs Mackay had gone to the far north. The green door (entrance from the garden to the back veranda and back door) no longer swung merrily on its hinges, giving notice to us in the schoolroom that Bachelor's Hall was occupied, and as day after day passed we used to wonder if our lives would be always so uneventful. Sometimes as we four girls sat on the hill by the flagstaff and looked out over the wide Pacific, we built castles in the air, and wove romances for the future. Dido's imagination, being always the most vivid. A change came all too soon, and although nothing startling ever happened, things were never the same to any of us again.

My mother had promised to visit her sister, Mrs Arthur Ranken, in September, at St Clair, her new home near Singleton.

In August Aunt Barbara invited Margaret and me to stay with her at Brownlow Hill while Uncle George was absent at his sheep station on the Murimbidgee. We had other invitations, especially one from Mrs Ranken at Saltran, and from my aunt that we should join mamma at St Clair. So, quite unexpectedly it was decided that we three should go together to Sydney in the little schooner, *Mary Ann*. I little thought then that dear Lake Innes would never be my home again. I re-visited it once only, five years afterwards.

Appendix

I

ANCESTORS
AND
EARLIEST
RECOLLECTIONS

[Reassembled from the opening pages of the original
Early Recollections and Gleanings, from an Old Journal]

GRANDMAMMA INNES had six daughters and ten sons. Of these one son and one daughter died young. The two eldest sons were soldiers, and were killed in battle before the birth of the two youngest girls, who were named for them, Gordonia (Gordon) and Williamina. John, the third son, died of consumption, and his mother then insisted on Robert, the fourth, who had become a soldier, retiring from the army. He did so, and lived and died at Thrumster. He married Henrietta Wemyss, and had an only daughter, who succeeded him.

In 1815 a blank commission was sent to my grandfather for any of his family. He determined that Archibald, the sixth son, a boy at school in Aberdeen, should accept it. I have often heard my uncle tell how he was brought home, measured for his uniform, hurried up to London, and before his fifteenth birthday was a month passed, found himself on his way to Belgium to join the forces under Wellington, and arrived at Waterloo the day after the battle had been fought and won, "just too late," he always added, regretfully. James, the fifth son, was a doctor. He married a Miss Macleod, and left one son and three daughters. The son is now General Macleod Innes, V.C., R.E. The seventh son died young. My father was the eighth; the ninth, Peter, lived to be a General and died unmarried; the tenth, Hugh, a promising young man, died of consumption. Of these ten sons, two grandsons only lived to grow up, so the Inneses are not an increasing family; and my grandmother's brothers, Clunes, have not left a single descendant.

Of my six aunts, the eldest, Anne Clunes, outlived all the other members of the family, and died at Thrumster in 1883, aged eighty-six. Aunt Jane died at Bletchingley, Surrey. She is buried at Godstone, where also rests her sister Barbara, wife of Sir George Macleay, K.C.M.G., of Pendell Court. He was knighted after her death. He erected a lovely monument to her memory in Godstone Church. Margaret died young, and Gordina [*sic*] when eighteen years of age. Williamina, the youngest, married Mr James Greg, and died at Tours, France, leaving three sons and three daughters. The youngest, Marie, married Captain Charlot, a French officer, and has several children, the others all died without having any family.

My grandfather Campbell's family property of Lochend, on Lake Menteith, was sold by his father, who bought the small estate of Inistore, near Appin, in Argyllshire, and called it Lochend. He married Margaret Fogo, who was aunt of Sir John Moore. My grandfather, John Campbell, was their eldest son.

.   .   .   .   .   .

When they left Skye [Kingsborough House, in Skye, where he and his wife spent the first years of their marriage] my grandfather took with him to Lochend as a household treasure an old-fashioned mahogany writing table which the Prince was said to have used when at Kingsborough. This table he took to Australia, and after many long journeys and strange adventures it was brought back to Scotland in 1865 by me, and is now at Garrallan, Old Cummock. He had also a tartan coat of Bonnie Prince Charlie's, which, unfortunately, was left in a cabinet or old chest of drawers that was sold unopened after he left Lochend. The person into whose hands it fell cut up the coat and distributed the pieces: a small piece only has been recovered by a member of the family.

My grandmother was the second daughter of Col. John Campbell of Melfort, in Argyllshire. Her father was a soldier of some distinction, and was for several years Governor or Commandant of Fort George, where a strong garrison was kept after the Rising of '45. He married somewhat late in life a very young girl, Colina, daughter of John Campbell, Auchalader, Perthshire. It is told of her that when her first baby was born she was still so fond of

Annabella Boswell and her family.

her doll that one day she was standing with it at the open window when her husband looked up from below, and naturally supposing it to be the baby, he called to her to be careful. Her answer was—"Here, catch it," at the same time throwing the doll out. The poor man grasped at the supposed infant unsuccessfully, and fainted on seeing it fall at his feet. We must, however, believe that this youthful bride made a good wife and mother, notwithstanding her childish beginning, for of her nine sons one was General Sir Colin Campbell, another Admiral Sir Patrick Campbell. Three were brave soldiers who were killed in Indian wars. The youngest son was General F. Campbell, who held important appointments at Wool-wich, and died there in 1866. Five of her daughters married, and two of them died unmarried at Hampton Court Palace.

I have heard my mother say that when the family started from Lochend on their distant journey [to Australia], their first stage was to Inveraray, from whence they cossed to St Catherine's, and travelled to Loch Goilhead in a coach, thence by boat to Glasgow. From Glasgow they went to Edinburgh by the canal, and from Edinburgh to London by sea, in what was then called a Leith smack, a comfortless little coasting vessel, and finally embarked in May 1821, for Tasmania, then only known as Van Diemen's Land, and a penal settlement. My grandfather and Mr George Ranken chartered the ship in which they sailed, and, in addition to their own families, took a few passengers and retainers. The Captain also took two or three passengers, and had his wife on board, so that there were several conflicting interests which helped to enliven the voyage, and to make it less tedious, if also at times not quite so agreeable as it might have been had the party been differently constituted.

The *Lusitania* put in at St Jago, where all enjoyed a delightful time and made many pleasant excursions, enjoying especially the fruit and flowers so abundant in that fine climate. I have now in my possession a few pretty little shells picked up at that time by my dear mother and long treasured by her. My grandfather's party received great attention from the American Consul, who was much fascinated by one of their number. No especial incidents marked the voyage after leaving St Jago, but of course, when crossing the line, all the old-fashioned ceremonies attending the visit of Neptune to the strangers on board were carried out, in some cases rather roughly. A warm and life-long friendship began on the voyage between my mother and Mr and Mrs George Ranken. They were but then newly married, a handsome young pair, full of life and energy. He was a son of Mr Ranken, of Glen Logan, Ayrshire.

My grandfather's family party consisted of his eldest daughter, Mrs Macleod, her husband, and three children, three grown-up daughters and a little girl, and four sons under fourteen. Not one of that party ever saw home again but my mother. Three older sons were soldiers in India, and one little boy was left in Scotland. He followed afterwards with his foster-mother, and was drowned when bathing while still a child. Of the three soldier sons two died early in their career. The eldest, General Sir John Campbell, C.B., outlived all the rest of the family except his youngest sister. He died in Edinburgh in 1878. All my other uncles and aunts died in Australia, and most of them had large families. I may here refer to Miss M. O. Campbell's book on the Campbells of Melfort, in which there is at least an outline of the family and of their descendants. The voyage lasted more than six months, so that Christmas was approaching when the *Lusitania* arrived at Hobarttown, and very thankful the weary passengers were to find themselves on terra firma.

My mother has often spoken of the beauty of the place and their delight at being established for a time at Restdown (now Reston), near Hobart, while my grandfather went on to Sydney with Mr Macleod, the Rankens, and other passengers. They there took up grants of land, which in those days were freely offered by the Government to all free emigrants desirous of settling in the colony. This being the case, on my grandfather's recommendation several of those who went out in his service received small grants of land, and some of their descendants are now wealthy and influential people, having been much more successful than any of his own family. Mr Macleod rejoined his family in Van Diemen's Land. They went to Norfolk Island for a time, then to New South Wales in 1835, and finally settled in Gipp's Land.

My grandfather's grant was situated near Parramatta, then a small settlement or town-ship called Rosehill, about fifteen miles from Sydney. He retained the native name of Bungarrabee. He there built a house and established a dairy farm, receiving from Government as many assigned or convict servants as he required. A certain number of cows were handed over to him till he was able to provide what was necessary for carrying on the establishment. This he was to do by breeding and buying, the arrangement being that after a term of years the same number of cows was to be returned as had been lent. At Bungarrabee,[1] he was joined by the rest of the family, and for a time all seemed to go well with them. . . . My grandparents did not live long to enjoy their new home: both died at Bungarrabee and are buried in Parramatta. After their death the place was sold and the family scattered.

2. To Speak for Myself

I have often heard discussions as to the time of one's life to which memory can go back, and to the certainty with which these early recollections can be depended on. For my own part I can remember one event before I was quite three years old, a very important one to me—the birth of my only sister—and a few incidents when I was four. Perhaps had these not been impressed on my mind by hearing them spoken of afterwards, they might have faded away, but from my fifth birthday I am certain of my own identity, and can follow the course of the events in which I have been interested or have taken any part, and from the time I was nine I have many old letters and journals with which to refresh my memory.

. . . . . .

Umbiella was the name of the station [at Capertee about sixty miles from Bathurst, to which the family moved from Yarrows, closer to Bathurst, in Annabella's infancy]. I have a sketch of it as it then looked, but have no recollection of having lived there. I have passed the place in after years, when it was a cattle station belonging to Sir John Jameson.[2] We were then living at Glen Alice, the adjoining station, which was a grant of land taken up by my uncle, Dr James Innes, who came from India, but who afterwards decided that he would not remain in Australia, and eventually

---

[1] The house has been demolished.

[2] Really Sir John Jamison, an important landholder and merchant. He arrived in the colony in 1814.

transferred the land to my father. From Umbiella we went to Parramatta in 1829 to stay with my uncle, Major A. C. Innes, who was Police Magistrate there. He had then quite recovered from a long and dangerous illness, through part of which in 1827 my mother had helped to nurse him with all the anxious care of a real sister. This kindness he always gratefully remembered, and during his whole life showed the affection and interest of a true brother in all that concerned her.

My earliest recollection is of his house, where in July 1829, my only sister was born. No doubt my impressions are all the clearer from having seen the place often in after years. I was then not quite three years old, and my first recollection of my dear mother was at this time. We went soon after to live in Sydney, where we had a pretty cottage in Princes Street,[1] with a deep veranda. In October 1829, my uncle was married to Miss Margaret Macleay, a daughter of the Colonial Secretary.[2] My baby sister, I have heard, was christened the next day, and named Margaret Clunes, after my uncle and new aunt: this also was the name of my grandmother Innes, they being the god-parents, and many years afterwards we found in her a kind and excellent friend.

I remember several events that happened during our residence in Sydney. The first was hearing of the death of King George the Fourth, and being immensely pleased at getting a new black sash. Another was finding one of the beads of a pretty cornelian necklace which I had broken and lost. Wishing to keep it safely, I pushed it into my ear. Fortunately I at once told what I had done, and my father rushed off for the doctor, and meeting his friend the doctor of the regiment then stationed in Sydney, brought him in. He happened to be in full uniform and was a most imposing individual, which probably is the reason of my remembering about the bead. It was also my first recollection of my father.

At that time we had frequent visits from a New Zealand Chief, Tagarouti by name, a tattooed warrior and very terrible to some people, but I was not at all afraid of him, and one of his companions was so great a friend of mine that on one occasion he went with us to the fruit market and there nearly brought us into great trouble. A man carrying a sack of corn or potatoes accidentally

[1] This street was destroyed for the building of the Sydney Harbour Bridge.
[2] Alexander Macleay: he became Colonial Secretary in 1826.

ANCESTORS AND EARLIEST RECOLLECTIONS

knocked me over, when the New Zealander rushed at him, and would have killed him had not the bystanders at once interfered. These men had come from New Zealand to Sydney with the Rev. Samuel Marsden, who was one of the first clergymen to devote himself to missionary work in New Zealand.

We did not live very long in Sydney. I next remember myself at Kiloshiel, near Bathurst, the home of my mother's great friends, Mr and Mrs George Ranken. We must have spent some time there, for I quite well remember my fifth birthday, 16th September 1831; and St Andrew's Day, the 30th November, on which day there was a great picnic of all the grown-up people of the district. Branches covered with cherries were cut from the trees that grew in the little garden in front of the house, and we children helped to pick a supply to be carried off in baskets. Some other days I remember we devoted to gathering quantities of roses to be made into rose-water and pot-pourri, the old-fashioned sweet-smelling English or cabbage rose. Mr Ranken had a small still, and was always trying experiments. His family then consisted of four boys and three girls —Jessie, the last, arriving during our stay with them. On my fifth birthday I was allowed to join the boys at their lessons, and got from their tutor my first copy book. In the afternoon we gathered flowers in the orchard, and, coming home, I tore some of the trimming off my new white frock, which grieved me much, as my mother had just embroidered it for me.

From Kiloshiel we went back to Capita to live, but not to our former station nor to Glen Alice, I don't know why. I think that Umbiella had been sold, and that the house at Glen Alice was not good enough; probably there was only a stockman's hut there, so we took up our abode at Warrangee. It was not a very nice place, though the new house was thought very good.

It was built of weather-board and shingled, and consisted of three rooms in a row, with three small rooms or skilleens. The old house or hut stood at right angles, built with slabs and covered with bark, and had three rooms also, but no skilleen. These rooms were a kitchen with a huge open fireplace, store, and the women-servants' room. The men lived in huts by the river some distance off. The end room of the house was the only room with a fireplace, and the only public room; the centre room was my mother's, and we two children occupied the little room off it; my uncles had the other room. We had at this time a very nice servant, who had been my sister's nurse, and our cook was a clever Irish woman, Kitty Coner by name, the wife of an old soldier who was then constable there. My father, being a district magistrate, always had one or more constables under him. Ann, our favourite, was going to marry our shoemaker, a very decent man; both were English, and both also were convicts. Ann leaving us was thought a good time for making a change in the household arrangements.

An immigrant ship was expected in Sydney—the first, I think, that brought young unmarried women to the colony. Two were at once secured for us. We children were no longer to be brought into contact with prisoner servants. We shed many tears at parting with our dear good Ann, but welcomed the new arrivals, who were to be so very superior. Such creatures they turned out, these "Red Rovers" as they were called from the name of the ship they came out in.[1] They were not a success, and those "True Patriots" who had left their country for their country's good were fearfully jealous of them. Of our two specimens, the one was full of airs and most objectionable; I do not know what became of her. The other speedily bestowed her affections on an old ticket-of-leave man, a sort of vet. or quack doctor, who made a fair living roaming through the country where he was known as the "karagee", the native name for the doctor or medicine man.

At Warrangee we had no fruit or flower garden, but on the banks of the river grew splendid melons and pumpkins. There, first the history of Cinderella stirred my childish mind to wonder, and I gazed upon the huge pumpkins with mingled awe and expectation.

We had among our men servants a poet, a genius—really quite a remarkable youth. Unhappily he never rose to the heights expected of him. He had much kindness and consideration shown to him, poor creature, but his motto alas was "Evil be thou my good". I shall only say of him at this time that during our stay at Warrangee he was bitten by a snake. He was of course brought up to the house at once, my mother being the best doctor within sixty miles. She had a good medicine chest, and books which she consulted, and had much experience and good common sense. On this occasion

[1] The *Red Rover* arrived in Sydney in September 1832. She had 202 women immigrants aboard.

she managed so successfully that the patient recovered, after keeping everyone up and in great anxiety for the whole night. I believe that brandy was poured down his throat, and he was made to walk up and down the whole night, kept on his feet by two men, otherwise he could not have been kept awake, being so drowsy and almost insensible.

Boucher was the name of another constable we had for a time— an old soldier who had been stationed at St Heleena just after Napoleon's death. He had many interesting things to tell of the time he spent there. Poor solitary old man, his memory has been kept green all these years by his gift to me of a little basket made from a cocoa-nut, which was elaborately carved. I still possess it, but the moss with which it was filled, and which Boucher himself had gathered from Napoleon's grave, has perished long ago.

One other recollection I must give of our time at Warrangee, the one that has most often come back to me. It is of the visit of Arch-deacon Broughton, afterwards the first bishop of New South Wales.[1] He was making a tour through some outlying stations and spent two nights with us. Everyone was invited to attend an afternoon service; it was held in the open air in front of the house. All our own people, of course, were present, and a few from the nearest station. The beautiful service was read most impressively and a short address given from the tenth chapter of Acts—St Peter's vision of the sheet let down from heaven containing all manner of creatures, the special lesson being that we should not despise any of God's creatures for he that feareth God and worketh righteousness is accepted of Him. I was only six years old, but I never hear or read these words without recalling that strange scene and congregation.

We must indeed have been rolling stones in those days, for our next resting place was Erskine Park, on the South Creek, not far from Liverpool. Here I spent my seventh birthday, September 1833. My sister was then a merry little girl of four, and many romps we had together. I cannot say that I remember our journey there. Probably we travelled from Warrangee in a caravan and camped out some nights on our way. In the spring we all made a grand expedition to the Woollombi by Windsor and Wiseman's Ferry. My youngest and only unmarried aunt was then staying with her sister, Mrs P. Grant Ogilvy, and the object of our journey was to visit

[1] The title is wrong: Broughton became the first and only Bishop of Australia.

Aunt Isabella and bring Aunt Anna back to Erskine Park with us. She lived after that chiefly with her brothers, till in 1837 she married Mr Arthur Ranken, now of Lockyersleigh,[1] near Goulburn, N.S.W. We had a charming journey, and slept several nights in the bush in or under our caravan. Never having revisited these places, I cannot attempt to describe the beautiful scenery, of which some remembrance haunts me as if seen in a dream. The lovely weather made our scrambles in search of ferns and wild flowers quite delightful, when we encamped for the night or rested at mid-day. I especially remember a great cabbage-palm or seaforthia which we carried back with us in triumph.

I have a little sketch of Erskine Park which serves to keep it fresh in my mind; it was done by Mr William Hardy, a frequent visitor and great favourite with us all. The house was a cottage with six rooms and a deep veranda, a plan very commonly adopted in those days. There were numerous out-buildings, a kitchen, dairy, servants' rooms, and stabling, the last of a rough and ready kind, as I found out one day to my cost. I was peeping through a broken weather-board to look at a new horse which had been with difficulty got into the stable. The creature kicked out a board which struck me in the face, and prevented any future wish on my part to visit that somewhat dangerous ground. I have since been told that my uncles had taken the place with the intention of forming a depôt for Valparaiso horses, which were at that time being brought to Sydney in great numbers, rough and unbroken, and there breaking them in. Some turned out well and brought high prices, which repaid the risk and loss on others. I do not think this speculation was a paying one. There was also a dairy, chiefly to supply butter to the Sydney market. The house was situated on rising ground: opposite, at some distance, was Bailey Park, and the South Creek ran in the valley between. On a hill at the back of the house were many wattle-trees; we used to gather quantities of fine pale gum from these. The place was overrun with a hateful plant known to us then as the cotton-tree.

About this time it was decided that I should be sent to school. I cannot remember that the prospect either pleased or troubled me. We had begun lessons regularly at Warrangee; our mother taught us, and I could write very well and was altogether rather precocious.

---

[1] Lockyersleigh still exists, but an upper storey has been added to it.

My parents were returning to Capita with the intention of settling permanently at Glen Alice, but the house they were building was still unfinished, and they could not accommodate a governess, so they took only my little sister with them to their new home.

Early in 1834 I found myself settled at school in Bridge Street, Sydney. . . . [From this point onwards the original sequence of the Journal is followed in the present edition.]

Appendix

II

THE RECONSTRUCTION DRAWINGS OF LAKE INNES HOUSE

LATE IN 1956 a friend who had just returned from a holiday at Port Macquarie showed me some photographs of the ruins of a house situated a few miles south of the town. These photographs were enough to arouse my interest and, at the end of that year, I paid my first visit to Lake Innes. Little did I realize at that stage how much I would become interested in the story of the Innes family or how much work I was blissfully and ignorantly accepting.

My primary purpose in visiting Lake Innes was to measure as fully as possible what remained of the house with a view to preparing accurate drawings of it as it once stood. Before my first visit I imagined that a couple of trips at the most should be sufficient to gather all information. Now, seven and a half years and many trips later, I have at last obtained enough information to prepare the drawings shown in this book. I must here point out that these drawings are not a complete reconstruction of Lake Innes House but are as complete as it is possible to make them. They have been prepared from measurements taken on the site as the basic source of information, together with old photographs and drawings of the house and descriptions left in Annabella Boswell's Journal helping to fill in where measurements were not possible.

The house stands on rising ground and is completely overgrown with lantana and another much more unpleasant plant known locally as Mysore Thorn, both of which were introduced by Mrs A. C. Innes. Large trees grow up from the centre of apartments and heavy layers of leaf-mould cover everything. Much of the ruins

216

have disappeared since my first visit, due mainly to the efforts of vandals and to the overwhelming jungle-like growth forcing its way through crumbling walls and eventually overturning them.

Early, in an effort to gather information, the Hastings District Historical Society cleaned all growth from the verandas, only to find on their next visit that all the paving stones had been stolen. After this it was decided to allow the undergrowth to spread and thus protect what was left from such acts of vandalism.

The first task I set myself was to measure and draw in plan everything that remained standing above ground and then with the aid of old drawings and photographs to reconstruct the elevations. This was all done with Annabella's Journal as constant reference.

When this work was completed it was found that no trace of the kitchen block, or the Bachelors' Hall, had been discovered. It was at this stage that a decision was made to turn archaeologist. It was assumed that whoever demolished these buildings would in all probability have left the section of walls below ground level untouched. This assumption was proved to be correct. By digging in the courtyard we found walls and steps in the position where the kitchen once stood. This course could not be adopted for the Bachelors' Hall, as apart from casual references to it by Annabella, nothing exists to pinpoint where to dig. Up till now no trace has been found of this building.

During the course of our investigations a couple of contradictions in evidence occurred. The first was concerning a fireplace in the drawing-room. Although the wall of the room remained standing there was no trace of the fireplace described by Annabella. Indeed, the wall appeared to be plastered for its full extent without any sign of where a chimney might have fallen. After I had examined two drawings of the house by different artists the fireplace was drawn in, as both artists agreed in showing a chimney at this place. I may add I drew the chimney on the elevations with great reluctance as it breaks every rule of composition usually so strictly adhered to by Georgian buildings.

The second contradiction involves the two artists mentioned above. Both show the house with an eaves overhang over the main walls of the house with a separate roof at a lower level over the verandas: yet a photograph of the house taken *circa* 1900 shows the main shingle roof sweeping down over the veranda. After I had checked

Lake Innes House.

levels of cement rendering to the external faces of the building the roof was drawn as shown in the photograph.

All timberwork on the house has of course long since disappeared. The details of the doors and columns shown are based on those of other houses built around 1830 and even though these may be incorrect in detail they are correct in character.

I should like to express my appreciation for assistance given by the Hastings District Historical Society members, particularly Mr and Mrs R. Howell of Lake Innes who carried out much spade-work in more senses than one.

To visit the ruins at Lake Innes is interesting; to visit it after reading Annabella's Journal is an experience. The place exudes atmosphere and it is very easy to imagine the younger members of the household doing the polka on the veranda or the piper playing in the early morning as described by Annabella in her charming journal.

RICHARD RATCLIFFE

RECONSTRUCTION DRAWINGS

S O U T H   E L E V A T I O N

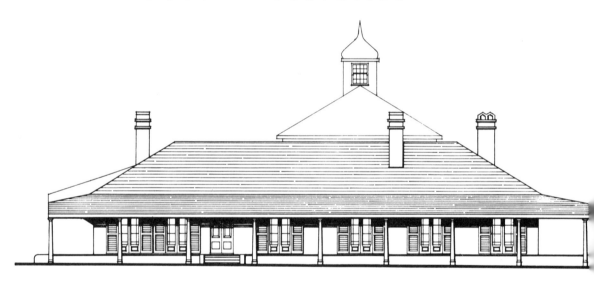

W E S T   E L E V A T I O N

Note ~ upper section of observatory block has been reconstructed from old drawings and may be inaccurate

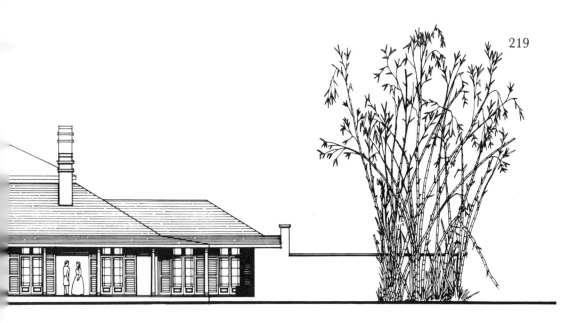

N O R T H   E L E V A T I O N

ELEVATIONS OF LAKE INNES HOUSE

From the reconstruction drawing by Richard J. Ratcliffe

RECONSTRUCTION DRAWINGS

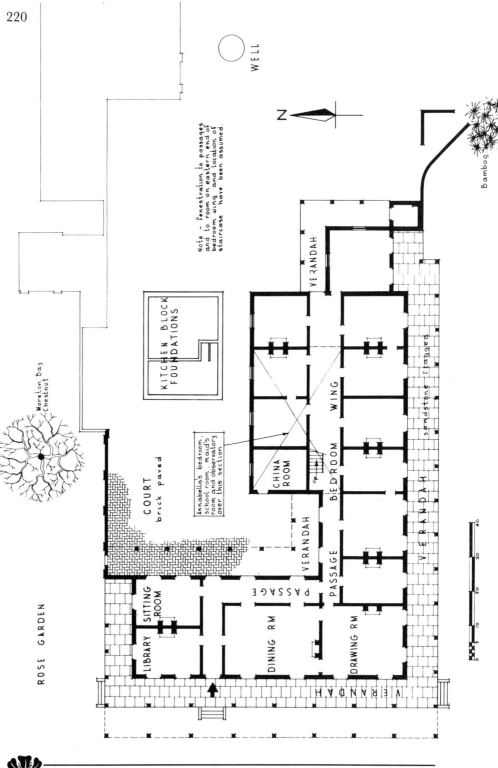

WELL

N

Bamboo

Note – fenestration to passages and to room on eastern end of bedroom wing and location of staircase have been assumed.

KITCHEN BLOCK FOUNDATIONS

Moreton Bay Chestnut

VERANDAH

Annabella's bedroom, school room, maid's room and observatory over this section

COURT brick paved

CHINA ROOM

BEDROOM WING

up

VERANDAH

PASSAGE

PASSAGE

sandstone flagged

ROSE GARDEN

LIBRARY SITTING ROOM

DINING RM

DRAWING RM

VERANDAH

VERANDAH

SHEET 1   PLAN OF THE MAIN BLOCK, LAKE INNES HOUSE

221

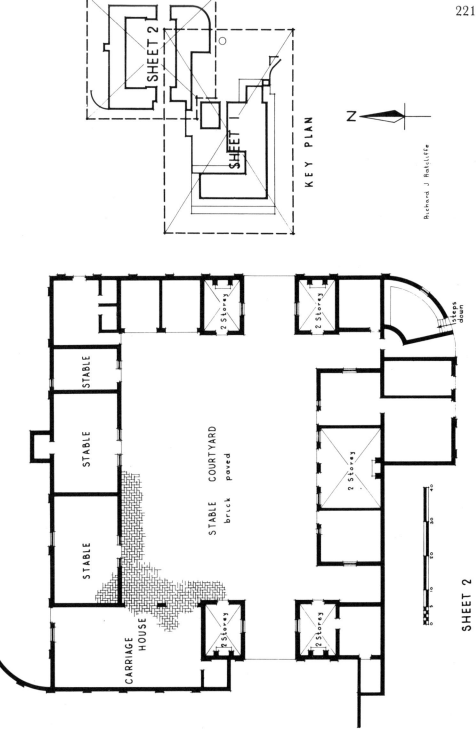

KEY PLAN

SHEET 2

SHEET 1

N

Richard J Ratcliffe

PLAN OF THE OUTBUILDINGS, LAKE INNES HOUSE

From the reconstruction drawing by Richard J. Ratcliffe

SHEET 2

STABLE

STABLE

STABLE

STABLE

CARRIAGE HOUSE

STABLE COURTYARD
brick paved

2 Storey

2 Storey

2 Storey

2 Storey

2 Storey

steps down

RECONSTRUCTION DRAWINGS